NATIONAL ACADEMIES *Sciences Engineering Medicine*

NATIONAL ACADEMIES PRESS
Washington, DC

Building Institutional Capacity for Engaged Research

Susan Debad, *Rapporteur*

Board on Science Education

Division of Behavioral and Social Sciences and Education

Proceedings of a Workshop

THE NATIONAL ACADEMIES PRESS 500 Fifth Street, NW Washington, DC 20001

This activity was supported by contracts between the National Academy of Sciences and the Bezos Family Foundation, National Aeronautics and Space Administration (Award #80HQTR24FA071), the National Institutes of Health (Award #75N98023P03171/002103), National Science Foundation (Award #2331516), The Pew Charitable Trusts (Award #37087), the Spencer Foundation (Award #202400101), and the William T. Grant Foundation (Award #ODF-204477). Any opinions, findings, conclusions, or recommendations expressed in this publication do not necessarily reflect the views of any organization or agency that provided support for the project.

International Standard Book Number-13: 978-0-309-73033-4
International Standard Book Number-10: 0-309-73033-3
Digital Object Identifier: https://doi.org/10.17226/28337

This publication is available from the National Academies Press, 500 Fifth Street, NW, Keck 360, Washington, DC 20001; (800) 624-6242; http://www.nap.edu.

Copyright 2025 by the National Academy of Sciences. National Academies of Sciences, Engineering, and Medicine and National Academies Press and the graphical logos for each are all trademarks of the National Academy of Sciences. All rights reserved.

Printed in the United States of America.

Suggested citation: National Academies of Sciences, Engineering, and Medicine. 2025. *Building Institutional Capacity for Engaged Research: Proceedings of a Workshop*. Washington, DC: National Academies Press. https://doi.org/10.17226/28337.

The **National Academy of Sciences** was established in 1863 by an Act of Congress, signed by President Lincoln, as a private, nongovernmental institution to advise the nation on issues related to science and technology. Members are elected by their peers for outstanding contributions to research. Dr. Marcia McNutt is president.

The **National Academy of Engineering** was established in 1964 under the charter of the National Academy of Sciences to bring the practices of engineering to advising the nation. Members are elected by their peers for extraordinary contributions to engineering. Dr. John L. Anderson is president.

The **National Academy of Medicine** (formerly the Institute of Medicine) was established in 1970 under the charter of the National Academy of Sciences to advise the nation on medical and health issues. Members are elected by their peers for distinguished contributions to medicine and health. Dr. Victor J. Dzau is president.

The three Academies work together as the **National Academies of Sciences, Engineering, and Medicine** to provide independent, objective analysis and advice to the nation and conduct other activities to solve complex problems and inform public policy decisions. The National Academies also encourage education and research, recognize outstanding contributions to knowledge, and increase public understanding in matters of science, engineering, and medicine.

Learn more about the National Academies of Sciences, Engineering, and Medicine at **www.nationalacademies.org**.

Consensus Study Reports published by the National Academies of Sciences, Engineering, and Medicine document the evidence-based consensus on the study's statement of task by an authoring committee of experts. Reports typically include findings, conclusions, and recommendations based on information gathered by the committee and the committee's deliberations. Each report has been subjected to a rigorous and independent peer-review process and it represents the position of the National Academies on the statement of task.

Proceedings published by the National Academies of Sciences, Engineering, and Medicine chronicle the presentations and discussions at a workshop, symposium, or other event convened by the National Academies. The statements and opinions contained in proceedings are those of the participants and are not endorsed by other participants, the planning committee, or the National Academies.

Rapid Expert Consultations published by the National Academies of Sciences, Engineering, and Medicine are authored by subject-matter experts on narrowly focused topics that can be supported by a body of evidence. The discussions contained in rapid expert consultations are considered those of the authors and do not contain policy recommendations. Rapid expert consultations are reviewed by the institution before release.

For information about other products and activities of the National Academies, please visit www.nationalacademies.org/about/whatwedo.

PLANNING COMMITTEE FOR WORKSHOP ON BUILDING INSTITUTIONAL CAPACITY FOR ENGAGED RESEARCH

SUSAN D. RENOE (*Chair*), Associate Vice Chancellor, University of Missouri
ELYSE L. AURBACH, Director for Public Engagement and Research Impacts, University of Michigan
TIMOTHY K. EATMAN, Inaugural Dean of the Honors Living-Learning Community, Rutgers University–Newark
ELSA FALKENBURGER, Director of the Community Engagement Resource Center, Urban Institute
MAHMUD FAROOQUE, Associate Director of the Consortium for Science, Policy and Outcomes, Arizona State University
KIMBERLY L. JONES, Associate Dean for Research and Graduate Education, College of Engineering and Architecture, Howard University
EMILY J. OZER, Professor and Faculty Liaison to the Executive Vice Chancellor and Provost for Public Scholarship and Engagement, University of California, Berkeley
BYRON P. WHITE, Associate Provost for Urban Research and Community Engagement, University of North Carolina-Charlotte

Staff

HOLLY G. RHODES, Project Director
SAMUEL CRAWFORD, Research Associate
BRITTANI SHORTER, Senior Program Assistant
HEIDI SCHWEINGRUBER, Board Director

BOARD ON SCIENCE EDUCATION

SUSAN R. SINGER (*Chair*), President, St. Olaf College
SUE ALLEN, Maine Mathematics and Science Alliance
MEGAN BANG, Professor of Learning Sciences, Northwestern University
VICKI L. CHANDLER, Provost, Minerva Schools at Keck Graduate Institute
KIRSTEN ELLENBOGEN, President and CEO, Great Lakes Science Center
MAYA M. GARCIA, Chief Program Officer, Beyond100K
DAVID GOLDSTON, Director, Massachusetts Institute of Technology Washington Office
G. PETER LEPAGE, Andrew H. and James S. Tisch Distinguished University Professor of Physics, Emeritus, Cornell University
WILLIAM PENUEL, School of Education, University of Colorado Boulder
STEPHEN L. PRUITT, President, Southern Regional Education Board
K. RENAE PULLEN, K–6 Science Curriculum Instructional Specialist, Caddo Parish Schools, Shreveport, Louisiana
K. ANN RENNINGER, Dorwin P. Cartwright Professor in Social Theory and Social Action, Swarthmore College
FRANCISCO RODRIGUEZ, Chancellor, Los Angeles Community College District
MARCY H. TOWNS, Bodner-Honig Professor of Chemistry, Purdue University
DARRYL N. WILLIAMS, Senior Vice President, Science and Education, The Franklin Institute

Staff

HEIDI SCHWEINGRUBER, Director
AMY STEPHENS, Associate Director
KERRY BRENNER, Senior Program Officer
SAMUEL CRAWFORD, Research Associate
KENNE DIBNER, Senior Program Officer
JANET GAO, Program Officer
LETICIA GARCILAZO GREEN, Research Associate
MARGARET KELLY, Program Coordinator
LUCY OLIVEROS, Senior Program Assistant
HOLLY G. RHODES, Senior Program Officer
LAUREN RYAN, Senior Program Assistant
BRITTANI SHORTER, Senior Program Assistant
TIFFANY E. TAYLOR, Program Officer
LACHELLE THOMPSON, Senior Program Assistant
AUDREY WEBB, Program Officer

Reviewers

This Proceedings of a Workshop was reviewed in draft form by individuals chosen for their diverse perspectives and technical expertise. The purpose of this independent review is to provide candid and critical comments that will assist the National Academies of Sciences, Engineering, and Medicine (National Academies) in making each published proceedings as sound as possible and to ensure that it meets the institutional standards for quality, objectivity, evidence, and responsiveness to the charge. The review comments and draft manuscript remain confidential to protect the integrity of the process.

We thank the following individuals for their review of this proceedings:

EMILY JANKE, University of North Carolina at Greensboro
CHHAYA KOLAVALLI, Ewing Marion Kauffman Foundation
LAURIE VAN EGEREN, Michigan State University

Although the reviewers listed above provided many constructive comments and suggestions, they were not asked to endorse the content of the proceedings nor did they see the final draft before its release. The review of this proceedings was overseen by **STEPHEN LINDER**, Institute for Health Policy, the University of Texas Health Science Center at Houston School of Public Health. He was responsible for making certain that an independent examination of this proceedings was carried out in accordance with standards of the National Academies and that all review comments were carefully considered. Responsibility for the final content rests entirely with the rapporteur and the National Academies.

Acknowledgments

We wish to express our gratitude to the members of the planning committee for their expertise and the time that they volunteered to create a full and engaging agenda. We are grateful for the dedication, good humor, and creativity that they brought to developing activities that tapped the collective wisdom of everyone at the workshop. We also want to thank each of the speakers and panelists for their insights and contributions to the rich discussions at the workshop, and for their own work toward advancing engaged research. Thanks also to the participants at this workshop not only for attending and enriching the discussions but also for their collective efforts as individuals and leaders to build capacity for engaged research.

Finally, we wish to thank the sponsors who provided the support to make this event possible: the Bezos Family Foundation, The Pew Charitable Trusts, the National Aeronautics and Space Administration, the National Institutes of Health, the National Science Foundation, the Spencer Foundation, and the William T. Grant Foundation. We want to give special thanks to Angela Bednarek and Benjamin Olneck-Brown of The Pew Charitable Trusts for their help as boundary spanners of multiple networks and efforts for this workshop.

Susan D. Renoe, *Chair*
Planning Committee on Building
Institutional Capacity for Engaged Research

Holly G. Rhodes, *Senior Program Officer*
Board on Science Education

Contents

Acronyms	xvii

1 Introduction   1
OPENING REMARKS, 2
ORGANIZATION OF THIS PROCEEDINGS, 3

2 The Importance of Engaged Research   5
CROSSING THE DIVIDE: LEARNING FROM A
    DISCONNECTED NEIGHBORHOOD, 6
COMMUNITY-BASED PARTICIPATORY RESEARCH
    FOR HEALTH, 7
BUILDING A WORKFORCE DEVELOPMENT SYSTEM
    FOR BOSTON'S YOUTH, 9
DISCUSSION, 10
Evolution of Research Questions, 11
Overcoming Barriers and Challenges, 11

3 Challenges and Solutions: Synthesizing Two Landscape Reviews   13
TENSIONS AND ACTION POINTS:
    A "MODEL OF SCALE", 14
Reform Faculty Evaluations, 14
Establish Intervention Points for External Funders and
    Build an Evidence Base, 16
LIMITATIONS OF SCANS, 17

4 Promising Approaches for Addressing Key Tensions in Community-Engaged Research   **19**

ADDRESSING TENSIONS RELATED TO VALUES, TRADITIONS, AND PRIORITIES, 19

Morehouse School of Medicine: An Institutional Commitment to Community Engagement, 20

University of California, Davis: A Systems View of Change to Foster a Culture of Engagement, 22

Brown University: A New Cabinet-Level Position to Advance Community Engagement Across the Institution, 23

Discussion, 25

ADDRESSING TENSIONS RELATED TO INFRASTRUCTURE, 27

Engage for Equity PLUS Model, 27

University of Pittsburgh: A Place-Based Approach to Engagement, 29

Three Concepts for Infrastructure Change: Challenging Norms, Organizing, and Operationalizing, 30

Addressing Pain Points, 31

Competencies and Capacity for Researchers, 32

Capacity Building for Communities, 33

Communication and Knowledge Exchange, 33

COMMON THEMES AND GAPS, 34

Understanding Existing Structures, 34

Financial Barriers, Funding, and Risk, 34

Using Data and Shared Language, 35

Reflective Practices and Global Perspectives, 36

Leveraging Cooperative Extension Systems, 37

Focus on Generating Solutions: Ideas from Workshop Participants, 37

5 Aligning Mission and Incentives: Valuing and Prioritizing Engaged Research   **39**

QUALITIES OF AN EXCELLENT INSTITUTION, 40

Prioritizing Community Involvement, 40

Innovative Promotion and Tenure Processes, 40

Agility, Adaptability, and Responsiveness, 41

LESSONS FROM THE NATIONAL INSTITUTES OF HEALTH MODELS FOR FUNDING COMMUNITIES DIRECTLY, 42

CHANGING EVALUATION: LEVERAGING DISCRETIONARY MOMENTS, 43

BUILDING CAPACITY FOR INNOVATION AND ENTREPRENEURSHIP, 44

THE ROLE OF PROFESSIONAL ORGANIZATION REQUIREMENTS IN ENCOURAGING ENGAGED RESEARCH, 44
Carnegie Elective Classification, 44
The Role of the Association of American Universities in Promoting Engaged Research, 45
INVESTMENTS FOR SUSTAINABLE ENGAGED RESEARCH, 46
DISCUSSION, 46
Time Constraints, 46
Improving Measurement of Engaged Research, 47
Sustainability, 48
The Role of Legislation, 48
INSIGHTS FROM KEY LEADERS, 48

6 **Valuing Diverse Forms of Expertise**   **51**
SHIFTING DYNAMICS OF EXPERTISE IN RESEARCH-PRACTICE PARTNERSHIPS, 52
CENTERING COMMUNITY EXPERTISE IN RESEARCH PARTNERSHIPS, 53
VALUING EXPERTISE AT SCALE, 54
BUILDING COMMUNITY CAPACITY FOR AGENCY, 55
DISCUSSION, 56
Challenges in Co-Design and Funding, 56
Entry Points for Engaged Research, 56
Revolutionizing Scholar Training, 57
Measuring Success by Community Impact, 57
Evolving Ethical Standards for Community-Engaged Research, 57
Addressing Skepticism, 58

7 **Aligning Core Values and Measurements**   **59**
ENGAGING COMMUNITIES AND CO-DEVELOPING A MEASURE OF TRUST AND TRUSTWORTHINESS, 59
Characteristics of Successful Engagement, 59
Project ENTRUST, 61
PARTICIPANTS' IDEAS FOR MEASURES, 62

8 **Next Steps for Action**   **65**
DISCUSSION, 66
Modeling Civic Engagement in Education, 66
Redesigned Funding Models, 67
Redesigned Institutional Structures and Epistemic Justice, 67

NEXT STEPS FOR INCREASING COORDINATION AND
        CAPACITY BUILDING, 68
  Building Scholarship and Equipping Individuals and Partners, 69
  Organizational and Culture Change, 69
  Artifacts, Metrics, and Incentives, 70
  Funding for Research and Sustainability, 71

Appendix A Workshop Agenda   73

**Appendix B Biosketches of Planning Committee
Members and Speakers**   79

Appendix C Participants' Ideas for Metrics of Engaged Research   93

Boxes, Figures, and Table

BOXES

1-1   Statement of Task, 2
1-2   Working Definition of Engaged Research, 3

3-1   Actions Needed to Advance Engaged Research by Level, 15

FIGURES

2-1   Community involvement in research, 8

4-1   The Morehouse School of Medicine T^{x}™ model, 21
4-2   Ecosystem for positive impact at Brown University, 24
4-3   Engage for Equity PLUS process, 28

TABLE

4-1   Core Competencies for Engaged Researchers, 31

xv

Acronyms

AAU	Association of American Universities
C2C	Community-to-Community
CAPHE	Community Action to Promote Healthy Environments
CIPHER	Computational Intelligence to Predict Health and Environmental Risks
NIH	National Institutes of Health
NSF	National Science Foundation
OSU	Oregon State University
PAR4 FED	Participatory Action Research for Fed Success
PTIE	Promotion & Tenure – Innovation & Entrepreneurship
SDG	Sustainable Development Goal
STEM	science, technology, engineering, and mathematics
SYEP	Boston's Summer Youth Employment Program
TIP	Technology, Innovation and Partnerships
UC	University of California
UNC	University of North Carolina
UNM	University of New Mexico

xvii

1

Introduction

The complex challenges facing society today call for new ways of doing research that bring researchers, policy makers, community leaders and members, industry stakeholders, and others together to identify evidence needs, contribute different kinds of knowledge and expertise, and use evidence to accomplish shared goals. Although momentum is building toward a research enterprise that more routinely enables and rewards this type of collaboration, the development of institutional capacities to support diverse forms of engaged research has not kept pace with the need for them.

Many universities have long made public engagement and impact central to their missions, including through extension programs at land-grant universities. However, barriers inside and outside of research institutions (e.g., institutional policies and structures, hiring and promotion policies, funding requirements, publishing pressures, and limited metrics to assess research impact) and at the individual level (e.g., professional preparation, time) make it challenging for scholars and partners to work together in mutually beneficial ways. Addressing these tensions and barriers can enable universities and other institutions to support diverse faculty; partner more effectively with communities, policy makers, and others; and, ultimately, mobilize research to contribute to more equitable societal outcomes. Fortunately, there are bright spots of innovation, and many research leaders, including government and private funders and university leaders, have already taken up the mantle of engaged and societally impactful scholarship, presenting a critical opportunity for key actors to align and coordinate their efforts.

BOX 1-1
Statement of Task

A planning committee of the National Academies of Sciences, Engineering, and Medicine (National Academies) will convene a 1.5-day workshop to bring together experts to propose areas for coordination and capacity building to advance engaged research. The sessions will highlight bright spots at learning institutions and in burgeoning networks. The workshop will explore key issues such as:

- Faculty incentives for engaged research and societal impact;
- Workforce capacity for engaged research, boundary spanning, and knowledge mobilization, including training and career paths;
- Institutional structures for engaged research, including university centers and think tanks;
- Measures and metrics for research impact and public engagement;
- Funders' and professional societies' role in supporting engaged research; and
- Linking initiatives across sectors, including within and outside government.

A proceedings of the workshop, summarizing the presentations and discussions, will be prepared by a designated rapporteur in accordance with institutional guidelines.

To capitalize on this opportunity, the Board on Science Education at the National Academies appointed a planning committee to design and host the workshop "Building Institutional Capacity for Engaged Research" in Washington, DC; it was held in-person and online on June 13 and 14, 2024.

In carrying out its statement of task, shown in Box 1-1, the planning committee convened a diverse set of leaders and stakeholders from across the research ecosystem to

- share actionable ideas and innovations that participants could use for building institutional capacity for engaged research institutions and settings, and
- propose concrete ideas for coordination and capacity building to advance engaged research.

OPENING REMARKS

Building the capacity to do the important work of engaged research cannot be achieved without a systems view and without engaging multiple

BOX 1-2
Working Definition of Engaged Research

Engaged research embeds rightsholder perspectives throughout the research life-cycle and encourages the production and use of knowledge in active collaboration with partners, including policy makers, practitioners, and communities.

sectors, said Susan Renoe, associate vice chancellor at the University of Missouri and chair of the planning committee. Forces both inside and outside of research institutions shape the capacity for engaged research, she noted, and multiple actors and sectors with a range of contexts and goals play varied and critical roles. In addition, taking concrete steps toward building institutional capacity for engaged research involves a willingness to view challenges as "tensions" instead of "impossible hard stops," she explained. Generating the actionable items necessary to move forward in building capacity involves examining the "bright spots" where innovation and progress are already occurring.

Acknowledging that there are a variety of terms for engaged research and related work, Renoe provided a working definition of engaged research, developed by the planning committee to guide discussions at the workshop: See Box 1-2. She noted that engaged research can involve a variety of methodologies, frameworks, and skills to appropriately engage partners in shaping research agendas for their needs. Agendas can be co-created with or grounded in the expertise that communities and other partners have and can foster uses of research to drive policy and practice to benefit society, added Renoe.

The workshop was designed to tap the collective wisdom of participants, Renoe said, encouraging deep participation and engagement in workshop discussions and activities. Workshop panelists and participants included leaders and engaged research champions in universities and other research institutions, communities, funding agencies, philanthropic organizations, publishing, and academic professional societies.

ORGANIZATION OF THIS PROCEEDINGS

Following this chapter's overview of the scope and aims of the workshop, Chapter 2 illustrates why building institutional capacity for engaged research is important, and Chapter 3 presents a synthesis of two landscape scans pointing toward potential solutions for tensions that have limited such capacity building in the past.

Chapter 4 highlights "bright spots" and innovative approaches to addressing tensions related to changing institutional cultures and infrastructures that limit engaged research. Chapter 5 features insights about how different sectoral actors can help to advance engaged research. Chapter 6 summarizes discussions about the cultural shifts needed to value diverse forms of expertise, and Chapter 7 focuses on ideas for advancing measurement of engaged research. The final chapter focuses on a future vision of engaged research and participant ideas for immediate next steps toward that vision.

The appendices provide the workshop agenda, biographical sketches of the planning committee members and speakers, and participant-generated ideas about measures of engaged research.

The workshop rapporteur has prepared this proceedings as a factual summary of what occurred at the workshop. The planning committee's role was limited to planning and convening the workshop. The views contained in the proceedings are those of individual workshop participants and do not necessarily represent the views of all workshop participants, the planning committee, or the National Academies.

2

The Importance of Engaged Research

The workshop began with the rationale for building capacity for engaged research, highlighting what can be achieved when societal impact and community needs are centered. According to a 2022 report by the Advisory Committee for Environmental Research and Education,[1] explained Kimberly Jones, planning committee member and associate dean for research and graduate education at the College of Engineering and Architecture at Howard University, engaging communities and other partners in research can

- enhance the relevance and increase the impact of science on society;
- broaden participation by increasing the number and diversity of stakeholders involved in the scientific process; and
- advance discovery, increase innovation, and improve product design.

Engaged research offers opportunities for both science and communities and other partners to benefit. A panel comprised of three teams of engaged researchers and their community partners illustrated how engaged research can benefit partners, researchers, and society. In a moderated discussion led by Jones, panelists also discussed factors that contributed to their successful collaborative work.

---

[1] Advisory Committee for Environmental Research and Education. (2022). *Engaged research for environmental grand challenges: Accelerating discovery and innovation for societal impacts.* National Science Foundation.

CROSSING THE DIVIDE:
LEARNING FROM A DISCONNECTED NEIGHBORHOOD

To showcase how engaged research can effectively address community needs, Jennifer Wilding, community development specialist for the Kansas City Federal Reserve Bank, and John James, president of the Wendell Phillips Neighborhood Association, described the Participatory Action Research for Fed Success (PAR4 FED) initiative—a project that ultimately benefited both the researchers and the community.

Wilding began by explaining that each of the 12 Federal Reserve banks has a Community Development Department that works to promote economic mobility in low-income and underserved communities. The PAR4 FED initiative was established in 2020 by the Kansas City Federal Reserve Bank's Community Development Department as part of their mission to encourage the use of engaged research to promote economic mobility in low-income and underserved communities. With the Urban Institute as a technical advisor, a pilot project was designed to address equitable broadband access—specifically, to determine why subscription rates remained low in some neighborhoods despite broadband access. The Kansas City Federal Reserve Bank partnered with the Wendell Phillips Neighborhood Association, the Kansas City Public Library, and aSTEAM Village,[2] an organization that helps young people move into the digital workforce. Together, they conducted a "data walk," a facilitated conversation to share the Federal Reserve Bank's research about broadband use in the neighborhood and to hear residents' perspectives about the accuracy and the implications of that research for the neighborhood. A report generated from these insights was published in 2023,[3] Wilding said. She noted two specific benefits of the partnership approach:

1. Community partners facilitated the connection between the Federal Reserve Bank and the neighborhood so that community members were comfortable with the partnership and did not feel like "the Fed had parachuted in."
2. Community partners were passionate and knowledgeable about the project's topic, and their active involvement represented an excellent resource, providing researchers with novel insights they may not otherwise have gained.

---

[2] See https://www.asteamvillage.org/

[3] aSTEAM Village, Federal Reserve Bank of Kansas City, & Wendell Phillips Downtown East Neighborhood Association. (2023). *Crossing the divide: What we learned from a disconnected neighborhood.* https://www.kansascityfed.org/Community/documents/9781/Broadband_data_walk_report_-_FINAL.pdf

To act on the study's findings, James and aSTEAM Village focused on addressing neighborhood needs while the Federal Reserve Bank shared the report with policy makers and participated in a research forum to enhance digital equity efforts. Highlighting the importance of the information gathered through community engagement, Wilding stated, "We are sure that we got a different reception than if we had only showed up with our maps."

James offered his perspective on the community benefits of this work and the factors that contributed to the project's success. Emphasizing that effective partnerships generate solutions or action items for all stakeholders, James said that the collaboration with the Federal Reserve Bank resulted in key deliverables including insightful data, a pathway to change, and tangible opportunities for the community. Specifically, because the data walk revealed inequitable access to broadband and a significant lack of trust in traditional broadband carriers, a cooperative with aSTEAM Village was subsequently developed to provide community-based broadband access— an outcome that supported both local economic growth and youth education. Furthermore, James reported, data that the Federal Reserve Bank shared with Missouri policy makers resulted in a grant to be used for digital literacy training in the community.

The partnership with the Federal Reserve Bank was participatory and empowering, James said. Reflecting on the experience as a community member being approached by researchers and the conditions needed to feel empowered in a research partnership, he reported, "When a community becomes a subject for research, we must come to the table with patience, and we must come to the table with interview skills because it is our job to determine what the baseline goal of researchers is and how the partnership can be successful for both sides." From the community's perspective, he continued, "settling in" to a partnership is facilitated by deep engagement in a project, beginning in its planning stages. "Neighborhoods are turned off by grant awardees that are just checking boxes on a checklist," he said, and instead are encouraged by "open discussion, to create an atmosphere where there is a possibility of an 'aha' moment that can happen on both sides of the table."

COMMUNITY-BASED PARTICIPATORY RESEARCH FOR HEALTH

Community involvement in research exists as a continuum, noted Amy Schulz, professor at University of Michigan School of Public Health, spanning key dimensions including shared power and control, responsibility and ownership, active participation, and decision-making influence: See Figure 2-1. Along this continuum, community involvement can range from investigator-driven studies to research that is fully community driven, she said, pointing out that community-engaged research is in the center of the continuum, given the range of ways such research can unfold.

FIGURE 2-1 Community involvement in research.
SOURCE: Adapted by the Detroit Urban Research Center from Ramsey (2008), as cited in Hacker, K. (2013). *Community-based participatory research*. Sage publications.

Emphasizing the evolution of her decades-long collaborative efforts with Angela Reyes, executive director and founder of the Detroit Hispanic Development Corporation, Schulz classified their work as employing a community-based participatory research approach, characterized by

- collaborative partnerships between academics and communities in all phases of the research project, including question development;
- emphasis on shared leadership;
- power sharing in the decision-making process;
- power building to address social inequities;
- commitment to translation of research to action;
- long-term commitment to partnerships;
- emphasis on accountability of funding and research institutions to the communities; and
- focus on equity in both partnerships and outcomes.

Schulz and Reyes have collaborated since 1995 on various long-term projects, ultimately founding the Community Action to Promote Healthy Environments (CAPHE) in 2013 to address air quality and health disparities in Detroit. The decades-long evolution of their collaborations, Schulz explained, highlights the importance of long-standing partnerships that transcend specific projects and demonstrate long-term commitment to the community. Most recently, these sustained relationships have spawned the Gordie Howe International Bridge Health Impact Assessment, aiming to measure and mitigate community health impacts of increased diesel truck traffic due to construction of a new international bridge at the Canada border crossing.[4] That project principally affects economically disadvantaged, predominantly Latino and African American communities. As both an affected community member and a member of CAPHE, Reyes used CAPHE's air quality data to assist in successful negotiations with various government entities, resulting in government-sponsored health impact assessments on nearby residential communities to address and mitigate the anticipated increase in air pollutants.

BUILDING A WORKFORCE DEVELOPMENT SYSTEM FOR BOSTON'S YOUTH

Since 2015, the city of Boston has engaged in a research-practice partnership with Northeastern University to evaluate Boston's Summer Youth Employment Program (SYEP), said Rashad Cope, deputy chief for the City of Boston's Worker Empowerment Cabinet. SYEP—a leader in youth jobs regionally and nationally since the early 1980s—has employed upward of 7,000–10,000 youth with approximately 500–900 local employers every summer. The aim of the partnership with Northeastern was to evaluate SYEP to further improve workforce opportunities and equity, Cope said, a goal that required a reliable evaluator invested in city priorities.

Alicia Modestino, associate professor at Northeastern University and research director for the Dukakis Center for Urban and Regional Policy, noted that the university's Community-to-Community (C2C) Impact Accelerator initiative, a $4.5 million investment in engaged research across Northeastern's 15 global campus locations, provides the critical infrastructure to support research-practice partnerships between researchers, policy makers, and practitioners, such as this partnership with the City of Boston.

The SYEP partnership with Northeastern University has resulted in several benefits for Boston, she said, namely the following:

- *Enhanced data collection*: Northeastern University provided invaluable expertise in data collection and evaluation, Cope said, which helped identify and address equity and capacity-building gaps in SYEP. Data enabled the city to refine workforce priorities and increase the efficiency of youth employment strategies.
- *Strategic alignment*: The partnership bridged gaps among the program's stakeholders, including employers and intermediaries. Coordinating efforts facilitated more comprehensive and cohesive workforce development strategies.

---

[4] See https://www.gordiehoweinternationalbridge.com/en/project-overview

- *Community benefits*: The partnership resulted in tangible benefits for many Boston neighborhoods, noted Cope, including navigation improvements in the online employment opportunity system, a placement algorithm to ensure equitable job assignments, and expanded grant opportunities for nonprofits to manage the employment program in their own organizations.
- *Additional programs and funding*: Survey and administrative data analyzed by Northeastern demonstrated that the Boston SYEP is "wildly impactful," Modestino reported: It improves employment and wage opportunities, increases high school graduation rates and access to college, and reduces involvement with the criminal justice system. This evidence, which was generated before the COVID-19 pandemic, spurred Northeastern and its partners to develop four new tracks of programming[5] that helped to keep youth employed during the COVID-19 shutdown. Research evidence was also used to justify a $4 million investment from the city to maintain youth employment at pre-pandemic levels and wages, she said.

In terms of the partnership's value for Northeastern, Modestino explained that she benefited as a researcher through regular interactions with Cope and the insights he provided from his years of experience running the program. The university also benefited through the opportunity to add value to the neighboring community rather than being extractive for purely research purposes, she said. Furthermore, both Northeastern University and the City of Boston benefited from a 2021 Institutional Challenge Grant of $650,000 from the William T. Grant Foundation to provide data and analysis to "build back better" post-COVID-19, across key areas that center the city's priorities.

To conclude, Modestino and Cope mentioned several main tensions experienced during the partnership, including the need to build staffing capacity in a tight labor market, changes faced during mayoral transitions, differing priorities between academic and municipal stakeholders, and the pressure and scrutiny they continue to face in producing data and insights to shape funding, resource, and logistical decisions.

DISCUSSION

The panelists described how their partnerships evolved over time and how they overcame the challenges they encountered.

---

[5] Programming included a virtual internship program and the Learn and Earn Program: https://www.boston.gov/departments/workforce-development/summer-learn-and-earn-program

Evolution of Research Questions

All the teams noted that the direction and focus of their research evolved through their collaborative work. Wilding and James explained that, based on the information collected during the data walk, their project shifted focus from the lack of interest in broadband to viewing the issue as one of equitable access, particularly in terms of such essential functions as education and telehealth. Schulz and Reyes also stated that community involvement influenced their research, helping to ensure their questions were relevant and beneficial to the community.

Sometimes, Reyes said, "it may be just a question of answering what the community is interested in first, and then going secondarily to the research question that the researcher was interested in. So, it's a process of negotiation and that equitable relationship, and co-learning." Modestino added that an annual research agenda-setting practice helped her partnership prioritize research questions that balanced scientific rigor with real-world needs. Cope expanded on Modestino's observation, noting that research aiming to create or change policy begins with "digging into what's happening on the ground[, which] leads to an iterative process. As you explore further, both the situation and questions evolve continuously."

Overcoming Barriers and Challenges

Panelists described four barriers they most frequently encountered in doing engaged research together:

1. *Training, coaching, and mentoring*: The time-consuming and emotionally draining nature of engaged work necessitates long-term institutional support, noted Modestino. For example, during the C2C program, her most significant unanticipated challenge involved the coaching and mentoring of faculty doing community-engaged work. Reyes and Schulz echoed the need for institutions to provide faculty training and mentoring, and Reyes called attention to the Detroit Urban Research Center's community-based participatory research training programs,[6] which create networks of support for both academics and community members. Wilding similarly noted the success of pilot projects in which the Kansas City Federal Reserve Bank participated, which built her team's engaged research skills and increased their comfort level as researchers.

2. *Tenure and promotion*: Several panelists noted the need to shift tenure and promotion criteria away from traditional metrics, such as

---

[6] See https://detroiturc.org/programs-expertise/cbpr-partnership-academy

peer-reviewed journal publications, to societal impact. A coordinated change across institutions is necessary, Modestino said, to boost the value of community-engaged work when soliciting external letters from other institutions and thus provide researchers the incentives to participate.

3. *Financial*: Several panelists cited financial barriers to engaged work, including the need for ongoing funding beyond traditional grant cycles. Community partner funding was noted as a specific challenge: "Universities are really only willing to support their researchers, while their policy partners are expected to do this work based on their institutional salaries or their blood, sweat, and tears," Modestino said, noting the lack of grant-making opportunities that could provide policy partners with financial support equal to the funding received by researchers.

4. *"Overresearch"*: James described the difficulty of being inundated by researchers approaching the community with research ideas. To overcome this challenge, researchers need to take the community's experience into account, he said, while the community also has a role to play: "You have to step back and give that researcher some grace as well, to say that 'I know what your point is. Let me see, as a community, how we can both achieve success together.'"

3

Challenges and Solutions: Synthesizing Two Landscape Reviews

Building institutional capacity for engaged research has multiple inherent challenges. To frame a comprehensive understanding of these tensions and kickstart participants' efforts to collectively address them, two members of the planning committee presented a synthesis of two recent landscape scans. Elyse Aurbach, director for public engagement and research impacts at the University of Michigan, and Emily Ozer, a clinical and community psychologist and professor of public health at the University of California, Berkeley, and the faculty liaison to the executive vice chancellor and provost on public scholarship and engagement, explained that the scans aimed to provide examples of ongoing efforts and promising avenues for action in overcoming institutional barriers and tensions.

Ozer detailed a national scan described in the white paper *Scan of Promising Efforts to Broaden Faculty Reward Systems to Support Societally-Impactful Research*,[1] which focused on identifying innovations in university faculty evaluation systems to recognize and reward societally impactful research. The scan, commissioned by participants in the Transforming Evidence Funders Network and published by The Pew Charitable Trusts, included several components: illustrative cases across 13 diverse U.S. universities; reviews of relevant reports, higher-education literature, and websites; and interviews with university leaders. The scan's goal was to inform funder investments to catalyze shifts in culture and policies in universities and the broader research ecosphere.

---

[1] See http://bit.ly/pew-landscape-scan

The second scan, explained Aurbach, was an initiative called *Modernizing Scholarship for the Public Good*.[2] This scan was designed with two purposes: (a) to explore how various institutional contexts create more permissive, flexible, and supportive opportunities for engaged and equity-oriented scholars; and (b) to provide guidance and an action framework for university leaders to create environments that drive and support institutional change efforts. The three arms of the study's approach included a broad advisory group, an extensive literature review, and case studies to illustrate the change process and successful initiatives. Deliverables consisted of an action framework and a database of tactics organized into specific actions appropriate for various actors in the ecosystem.

TENSIONS AND ACTION POINTS: A "MODEL OF SCALE"

A combined view of the two landscape scans clarified common tensions and allowed Aurbach and Ozer to identify several actionable avenues to address those challenges.

Actions at three levels of scale are needed to address common tensions encountered when building capacity for engaged research, said Aurbach: the individual level, the research institution level, and the meta-network level. The landscape scan presented by Ozer spanned all three scales, with an emphasis on incentive systems and funders as the primary audience; in contrast, the scan Aurbach presented, aimed at institutional change leaders, was primarily focused on the individual and institutional levels. The action points synthesized from the collective work of the scans are shown in Box 3-1.

Reform Faculty Evaluations

Ozer provided additional insights from *Scan of Promising Efforts to Broaden Faculty Reward Systems to Support Societally-Impactful Research*. Faculty evaluations based on traditional approaches that undervalue engaged research were noted as a critical tension point in both landscape scans, she noted. Institutions need to develop new guidelines for faculty evaluation, she said, not just in terms of promotion and tenure but across entire careers. In addition, "guidelines are not enough," she said. "There is the bigger question about implementation [and] about enculturation—what's happening at the center of campus [and] what's happening in disciplines and departments."

---

[2] See https://www.aplu.org/our-work/2-fostering-research-innovation/modernizing-scholarship-for-the-public-good/

CHALLENGES AND SOLUTIONS

BOX 3-1
Actions Needed to Advance Engaged Research by Level

Individual Level: Equip academic and community partners with skills, resources, and knowledge bases to engage ethically, effectively, and equitably

- Establish competency frameworks for engaged faculty
- Incorporate engaged research skills into graduate education programs
- Empower community partners to "speak the language of academics"

Research Institution Level: Organize research institutions to create facilitative, supportive environments

- Amplify societally impactful scholarship as part of institutional identity
- Equip committed institutional leaders
- Invest in institutional structures and networks, including by actions that
    ◦ Reduce legal, regulatory, procedural, bureaucratic, and social barriers
    ◦ Strengthen within and cross-campus/organization networks and programs to accelerate innovation and impact
    ◦ Launch and maintain catalytic funding programs and sustained institutional investments
- Develop awards and other mechanisms to recognize and celebrate work
- Formalize student curricular training and professional development opportunities
- Reform appointment, retention, tenure, and promotion practices

Meta-Network Level: Energize the meta-network to shape the broader disciplinary and funding ecosystems to prioritize and support societally impactful research

- Build societally impactful scholarship into institutional identity
- Provide funding support to accommodate the time-intensive nature of partnered scholarship
- Elevate visibility for societally impactful scholarship
- Align assessment practices to evaluate impacts of engaged research

SOURCE: Workshop presentation by Elyse Aurbach and Emily Ozer.

Beyond evaluation guidelines, the scans identified several institutional innovations developed to recognize engaged research and other "atypical" forms of scholarship, including new committees, training to teach tenure and review boards to recognize atypical forms of scholarship, and capacity building to help candidates strengthen their cases during the evaluation process. "It's not one-size-fits-all," Ozer noted, highlighting that these innovations necessarily differ across university systems.

Establish Intervention Points for
External Funders and Build an Evidence Base

It is important not only for research institutions to build "societally impactful scholarship" into their institutional identities but also for other actors in the research ecosystem, including funders. Beyond research institutions themselves, external funders can advance engaged research by shaping the funding ecosystem to recognize and reward societally impactful research, noted Ozer. The scan she described identified several intervention points that could be leveraged by funders aiming to accelerate and increase the impact of engaged research:

- funding for the engaged research (including dissemination and application) that accommodates the time frames and time-intensive nature of partnered scholarship;
- funding to support institutional change makers in their work prioritizing, catalyzing, and embedding engaged research practices;
- funding to support systematic institutional change at universities as they tailor strategies and infrastructure, and as they work to broaden and sustain cultural changes including faculty evaluation policies;
- funding of convening opportunities to support institutional cross-learning, cooperation, and collaboration; and
- funding to strengthen the broader ecosystem.

Ozer expanded on these points, noting that funding is needed to provide resources for research generation, support its dissemination and application, and enhance the visibility, legibility, and prestige of such research in internal and external evaluation. Furthermore, funders, collective convening power can be used to encourage more substantial investments aligned with societally impactful scholarship, especially via cooperation and collaboration among funders, and to strengthen and uplift scholarly outlets for societally impactful research.

Ozer asked participants to consider factors important for building an evidence base of institutional change—namely, systematic processes and evidence of impact specific to various conditions, university contexts, and approaches. She asked the group to consider ways to establish "a holistic, multi-method review that 'sees' diverse forms of scholarship and indicators of excellence."

LIMITATIONS OF SCANS

While the two landscape scans presented may be useful for a broad understanding of ongoing efforts and promising avenues for action in engaged research, they have several important limitations, said Aurbach. Specifically, the scans do not

- cover the histories of how and why the academic systems evolved;
- identify specific opportunities for addressing multiple key areas of change, such as diversity, equity, and inclusion work or open science initiatives;
- address partnerships and how partnerships can differ across disciplines and sectors; nor
- address mismatches between mission and infrastructure that can undermine trust, effectiveness, and timeliness.

Overall, this workshop session emphasized the importance of community-engaged research, focusing on the ability of this method to enhance the relevance, inclusivity, and societal impact of research studies. Landscape scans provided the foundation for a deeper dive into the key tensions faced by engaged researchers and promising approaches for addressing those challenges to advance engaged research practices across diverse institutional contexts.

4

Promising Approaches for Addressing Key Tensions in Community-Engaged Research

In pursuing engaged research, institutions often encounter tensions related to differing values, traditions, and priorities. This chapter explores promising approaches developed by various universities and research organizations to address these challenges. Through case studies and discussions, panelists shared strategies for aligning institutional infrastructure with the needs of engaged research, fostering inclusive cultures, and overcoming barriers that impede progress. The chapter also highlights successful models implemented to navigate and resolve the inherent tensions between traditional academic structures and the demands of engaged scholarship.

ADDRESSING TENSIONS RELATED TO VALUES, TRADITIONS, AND PRIORITIES

Engaged research can often be at odds with the traditional structure of research institutions and with values held both inside and beyond those institutions, noted Mahmud Farooque, planning committee member, and associate director of the Consortium for Science, Policy and Outcomes at Arizona State University. Farooque highlighted the historical tension in American universities between the production of knowledge, or "science for science's sake," and the application of knowledge, noting the general belief that one comes at the expense of the other. Shifts in focus usually have been driven by some combination of technological opportunities, demand conditions, and policy choices, he said. For example, the U.S. National Science Foundation was established in 1950, which shifted universities away from use-inspired research to a more science-centric approach. Then, beginning

19

from the 1970s, economic and competitive pressures led to a renewed emphasis on the practical application of research, facilitated in the following decade by the Bayh-Dole Act,[1] which allowed universities, businesses, and nonprofit entities to own and commercialize inventions developed through federally funded research. Universities responded by establishing technology transfer offices and leadership positions focused on market-use-inspired research. Currently, there is a further shift in the knowledge-production mode, from "science *for* society," toward a community- and outcomes-focused mode, to "science *with* society"—a transition that is particularly difficult due to differences in values between the two approaches, Farooque acknowledged.

Farooque invited panelists to share their experiences building systems and cultures that support engaged research in their respective contexts and to discuss their approaches to addressing tensions around institutional values, traditions, and priorities.

Morehouse School of Medicine:
An Institutional Commitment to Community Engagement

"Community-campus relationships and trust in research are essential drivers for research that *matters*, both in terms of evidence-based rigor and impact but also the diffusion of those innovations between community-campus partners and the broader institution, which needs to learn how to do it and have that positive impact," said Tabia Henry Akintobi, professor and chair of community health and preventive medicine and associate dean for community engagement at the Morehouse School of Medicine. Morehouse—a historically Black medical college, invests in "relationships first," said Akintobi, with a focus on primary care and community-engaged research involving disproportionately impacted community and patient groups.

A key feature of Morehouse's engaged research infrastructure is a community governance board with bylaws and rules of engagement ensuring community members' involvement in all pillars of the institution, including serving on the board of trustees and institutional review boards. Within this infrastructure, communities are "critical, equitable partners [. . .] in really identifying what the research should be and why it is important," Akintobi said. Furthermore, community partners are strategically positioned to directly engage with funders, industry, and community leaders, she explained, to delineate issues and determine means to address them.

---

[1] Bayh-Dole Act, 35 U.S.C. § 200 *et seq.* (1981). https://www.govinfo.gov/content/pkg/USCODE-2011-title35/html/USCODE-2011-title35-partII-chap18.htm

PROMISING APPROACHES FOR ADDRESSING KEY TENSIONS 21

FIGURE 4-1 The Morehouse School of Medicine T^x™ model.
SOURCE: *T^x™: An approach and philosophy to advance translation to transformation.* https://www.msm.edu/Research/tx-health-equity/index.php

Morehouse's commitment to community engagement is evidenced by a trademarked research framework developed in 2016 called T^x™,[2] which emphasizes collaboration among health policy researchers, community partners, and clinical researchers across multiple areas of translational research: See Figure 4-1. According to Akintobi, the T^x™ model broadens the evidence base and leads to approaches that are adopted by or adapted to communities.

In addition to publishing this model, Morehouse provided $1 million, in $75,000 increments, to strategically identified researchers to advance T^x™ scholarship. The return on investment, Akintobi noted, has been about $75 million in funding from the National Institutes of Health and industry to these researchers and community partners. Akintobi also highlighted

---

[2] See https://www.msm.edu/Research/tx-health-equity/index.php; Akintobi, T. H., Hopkins, J., Holden, K. B., Hefner, D., & Taylor, H. A., Jr. (2019). T^x™: An approach and philosophy to advance translation to transformation. *Ethnicity & Disease, 29*(Suppl 2), 349–354. https://doi.org/10.18865/ed.29.S2.349

the Champions for Health Equity Curriculum, which helps to train other universities to build successful partnerships.

Akintobi concluded by emphasizing that Morehouse's strategic plan "has positioned community engagement as a pillar within our academic health center that's equitable and resourced just like pillars of clinical care, research, and education," providing engaged research with the resources needed to advance health justice.

University of California, Davis:
A Systems View of Change to Foster a Culture of Engagement

Using the analogy of "a slow rising but powerful upswell," Michael Rios, vice provost of public scholarship and professor of human ecology at the University of California (UC), Davis, shared the university's journey toward becoming a leader in engaged research and public scholarship. Following an incident in 2011 in which students were pepper sprayed by campus police and the elimination of community outreach programs in 2014, the university subsequently experienced a resurgence in interest in community engagement, mobilized by a group of faculty whose scholarship was increasingly at odds with traditional definitions of research. Within a 3-year span, Rios noted, the university attained Carnegie Foundation Elective Classification for Community Engagement,[3] became the host institution for Imagining America,[4] and established the Office of Public Scholarship and Engagement.[5] More recent progress includes investment in a university innovation district, initiation of an anchor institution strategy to address social determinants of health, local workforce development, and the creation of a Grand Challenges Office to organize research to holistically tackle complex, interconnected social or cultural issues.

Rios takes a systems view of change, he said, drawn from his diverse experiences in community engagement and urban planning and design and shaped by three main drivers of institutional capacity building:

1. The *where and when*: Context-specific opportunities are available in the institutional environment.
2. The *what and why*: A compelling vision exists that motivates individuals and groups to action.
3. The *who and how*: Mobilized action is structured around collaborative, inclusive processes to ensure lasting effect.

---

[3] See https://carnegieclassifications.acenet.edu/elective-classifications/community-engagement/
[4] See https://imaginingamerica.org/
[5] See https://publicengagement.ucdavis.edu/

The Office of Public Scholarship and Engagement, Rios described, acts as a scaffold to facilitate collaborations across different units, amplify the value and impact of this work, and advocate for institutional reforms. The Office of Public Scholarship and Engagement is guided by four institutional strategies implemented to cultivate and foster a culture of engagement that recognizes and rewards publicly engaged scholarship, builds collective impact of scholars, and increases UC Davis's impact:

1. reframing the narrative from community outreach to engagement, through a communications-based approach that emphasizes reciprocity and mutual benefit;
2. creating spaces of faculty recognition and inclusion and emphasizing public scholarship as an integral part of the university's research and teaching mission that is considered in merit and promotion processes;
3. aligning efforts with the university's priorities and strategic plan, and the priorities of high-level offices; and
4. expanding the ecosystem of engagement across UC Davis and the UC system, including a recent multiyear process to document and assess the impact of community partnerships and public impact and the formation of the UC Community Engagement Network.[6]

Rios concluded by noting that progress has been made on each of the four strategies,[7] including public scholarship engagements, programs, initiatives, and online resources.

Brown University:
A New Cabinet-Level Position to
Advance Community Engagement Across the Institution

Mary Jo Callan, vice president for community engagement at Brown University, discussed her role in coordinating the university's community engagement efforts since her position was established in 2022. She described the 260-year-old Rhode Island institution as unique due to its location in a small state with an interconnected community. This context of connection, said Callan, along with Brown's mixed local reputation and complicated history of both benefit and harm, spurred the university to strengthen its commitment to advance mutuality and positive impact across all community engagement efforts. As part of these efforts, Callan's cabinet-level

---

[6] See https://uccommunityengagementnetwork.org/
[7] See https://publicengagement.ucdavis.edu/

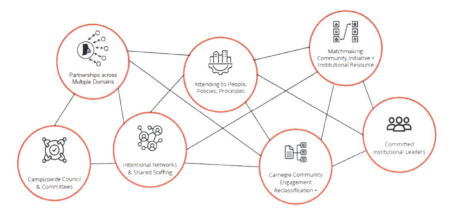

FIGURE 4-2 Ecosystem for positive impact at Brown University.
SOURCE: Workshop presentation by Mary Jo Callan.

role was created to advance mutuality and positive impact beyond engaged research, to encompass every aspect of the institution, as depicted in Figure 4-2.

"We are working to identify, make legible, and change policies and processes across the institution, in every domain, that inhibit sustained reciprocal positive engagement, including tenure, promotion, and reward," said Callan, noting additional strategies that include

- nurturing people and facilitating networks to reliably connect, coordinate, and support high-quality engagement;
- using a stakeholder-management system paired with dedicated matchmakers to facilitate understanding of community partner priorities and ideas and connect them with researchers who share those ideas;
- recruiting committed institutional leaders, as well as interested faculty and staff; and
- leveraging reclassification for the Carnegie Foundation Elective Classification for Community Engagement to deepen institutional commitments and drive systemic change.

"We're using every lever at our disposal, understanding that this is central to our excellence, our success, and our relevance," Callan said, referencing a recent institution-wide agenda that includes 80 strategies and actions.[8]

---

[8] See https://president.brown.edu/sites/default/files/2024-05/community-engagement-agenda-2024.pdf

PROMISING APPROACHES FOR ADDRESSING KEY TENSIONS   25

To conclude, Callan summed up Brown University's theory of change, which is premised on investments in partnership capacity:

> Through coordinated, collective action that draws on every aspect of the institution that centers our place—centers Rhode Island and quality of life—by connecting students, faculty, staff, and even alumni with community experts, health care providers, teachers, neighbors, [and] parents, and engaging every part of our institution, we can more fully and more clearly contribute to quality of life in Rhode Island. Engaged research is a huge part of this agenda. But again, we believe that situating and communicating it in its broader context will improve both our research and our institutional excellence.

Discussion

The discussions that followed the workshop presentations covered several topics related to the tensions panelists highlighted, including sustaining community engagement, participants' visions of a future engaged landscape, and the influence of intergenerational change in shifting engagement practices.

Sustaining Community Engagement

In identifying positive drivers for sustaining community engagement efforts, Akintobi emphasized the importance of positioning community and patient engagement to be "health topic agnostic"—beyond any particular research focus. To promote sustainability and health equity, engaged institutions need to serve as both resources and partners, addressing community issues while amplifying community leadership and power, she said. Three stakeholder groups are necessary for this effort: community and patient leaders engaged as senior partners, policy and agency leaders who can influence policy makers regarding funding decisions, and academic partners who ensure rigorous, evidence-based solutions. This comprehensive model removes the singular research focus and promotes health equity in ways that benefit multiple stakeholders, regardless of changes in institutional leadership, said Akintobi.

Rios echoed Akintobi's points, stressing that embedding engagement deeply in an institution's identity, not just in its research, can help ensure that engagement efforts persist beyond individual initiatives or leadership cycles. Such work requires "ownership and a constituency that is going to take that torch and diffuse it over time and space," he said, and grassroots support from faculty, students, staff, and community partners is critical for building an inclusive institutional culture. Callan added that both practice and visible success are crucial for establishing and maintaining a culture of engagement. Increasing the number of individuals participating in these joyful, rewarding efforts can help to shape and sustain a culture of engagement, she said.

Vision for a Future Landscape

To guide progress toward a landscape shift, a workshop participant asked panelists to project their future visions of university community engagement over the next decade. Callan's vision identified the important role of funding. While funders are exhibiting an increasing interest in financing engaged work, efforts are often disconnected at the institution level, which community partners can find exhausting and incoherent. To solve this problem, she emphasized funding coordinated community engagement mechanisms and infrastructure within and across institutions.

Akintobi envisioned a landscape focused on broader social and political determinants of health or "the barriers and facilitators to healthy living" as key areas for future engaged research and funding efforts. Such efforts could include workforce and economic development, he noted. Rios said his vision of the future includes erasing boundaries between universities and communities, with an emphasis on co-created knowledge and faculty evaluation systems that intrinsically recognize engaged research.

Attracting and Preparing Students

A question from one participant focused on whether institutions' efforts toward engaged research have attracted students. Akintobi observed that many of today's students are driven by a passion for justice and equity, and while they are motivated to engage in research, barriers around the rewards and benefits of academic work need to be reduced to retain them. Rios highlighted a doctoral student cohort program at UC Davis that fosters a sense of belonging among students across disciplines, preparing them for careers that benefit the public.[9] Many students involved in engaged research do not aim to become professors, he said, but instead seek to use their skills directly for the public good. Callan similarly noted that both undergraduate and graduate students at Brown are eager to engage and that engaged research often expands students' perspectives and enthusiasm, especially when driven by community partners.

Preparing the next generation of students for engaged research requires providing them with relevant expertise. A participant asked about translating research into policy and the role of institutions, including smaller institutions like community colleges, in equipping students with policy advocacy skills. Akintobi agreed with the need for such training, noting that it is often provided by community-based organizations. Callan concurred, noting that community partners are often the "credible messengers" needed for effective policy translation. Rios shared a practical approach from UC Davis, in which faculty fellows are required to write blogs to enhance their communication skills.[10]

---

[9] See https://publicengagement.ucdavis.edu/public-scholars-future
[10] See https://publicengagement.ucdavis.edu/reflections

ADDRESSING TENSIONS RELATED TO INFRASTRUCTURE

Farooque concluded the discussion by suggesting that the science of engagement could be advanced by capturing the experiences of people like those on the workshop panel, turning such experiences into scholarship to guide future efforts in community engagement.

ADDRESSING TENSIONS RELATED TO INFRASTRUCTURE

Another type of tension facing engaged research efforts involves challenges related to operational processes, procedures, or organizational structures. Elsa Falkenburger, planning committee member and a senior fellow at the Urban Institute and director of its Community Engagement Resource Center, moderated a panel discussion that highlighted actionable insights for modifying institutional infrastructure to achieve the bidirectional benefits of engaged research.

Engage for Equity PLUS Model

Prajakta Adsul, assistant professor in the Department of Internal Medicine at the University of New Mexico (UNM) and an affiliate member of the university's Center on Participatory Research, said that the frustration she experienced while performing community-engaged work in cancer prevention motivated her efforts in working with Engage for Equity.[11] The Engage for Equity model, which includes approximately 400 federally funded research partnerships nationwide, is based on previously identified community-based participatory research practices critical for generating meaningful outcomes, including a sense of "collective empowerment," shared governance, and shared principles common to models of community-based participatory research.[12]

In the course of that work, Adsul's team noted that many partnerships faced similar institutional barriers, such as institutional review board processes and other policies and practices that were not supportive. Engage for Equity PLUS,[13] a one-on-one coaching model for academic health institutions, aims to address these challenges, Adsul said. To scale up learning from the partnership level to the institutional level, a team of academics and community partners first assesses the institutional context using a

---

[11] See https://engageforequity.org/

[12] Duran, B., Oetzel, J., Magarati, M., Parker, M., Zhou, C., Roubideaux, Y., Muhammad, M., Pearson, C., Belone, L., Kastelic, S. H., & Wallerstein, N. (2019). Toward health equity: A national study of promising practices in community-based participatory research. *Progress in Community Health Partnerships: Research, Education, and Action, 13*(4), 337–352. https://doi.org/10.1353/cpr.2019.0067/

[13] Sanchez-Youngman, S., Adsul, P., Gonzales, A., Dickson, E., Myers, K., Alaniz, C., & Wallerstein, N. (2023). Transforming the field: The role of academic health centers in promoting and sustaining equity based community engaged research. *Frontiers in Public Health, 11.* https://doi.org/10.3389/fpubh.2023.1111779

mixed-methods approach, which involves engaging community members, researchers, staff, and institutional leadership. Data are then showcased back to the institution through workshops designed for iterative evaluation and collective reflection, and strategic priorities are set.

The Engage for Equity PLUS model was tested with three academic health institutions: Stanford University, the Morehouse School of Medicine, and the Fred Hutchinson Cancer Center. Preliminary results revealed several positive outcomes, Adsul said, including the recognition of both community and institutional leaders as members of a "champion team." As Figure 4-3 depicts, this team played a central role in the process of institutional change.

The model facilitated the creation of patient engagement offices that provided researchers with structured ways to collaborate with patients, and it addressed institutional review board processes, focusing on overcoming fiscal and administrative barriers to adequately compensating community partners. Adsul noted that ongoing work with the Mayo Clinic has led to further refinements, such as the development of a community-engaged research

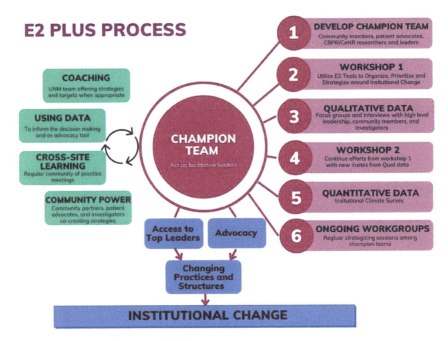

FIGURE 4-3 Engage for Equity PLUS process.
SOURCE: Sanchez-Youngman, S., Adsul, P., Gonzales, A., Dickson, E., Myers, K., Alaniz, C., & Wallerstein, N. (2023). Transforming the field: The role of academic health centers in promoting and sustaining equity based community engaged research. *Frontiers in Public Health, 11.* www.frontiersin.org/journals/public-health/articles/10.3389/fpubh.2023.1111779/full, under the terms of the Creative Commons Attribution License (CC BY).

PROMISING APPROACHES FOR ADDRESSING KEY TENSIONS 29

playbook and training for both researchers and community members. Teams also provided patients and engaged researchers with a common access point and matchmaking services, she noted. The model is currently being expanded to include eight additional clinical translational science centers, aiming to embed successful practices more broadly within diverse research institutions.

University of Pittsburgh: A Place-Based Approach to Engagement

While universities may address global issues, they are fundamentally place-based, meaning they are affected by and affect the regions in which they are located, stated Lina Dostilio, vice chancellor of engagement and community affairs and associate professor in the School of Education at the University of Pittsburgh. The evolution of the University of Pittsburgh, she explained, is inextricably linked to the socioeconomic and environmental legacies of western Pennsylvania. Dostilio pointed out that local disparities in this region create research opportunities for the university's engaged researchers—but traditional research methods often fail to translate data on people's experiences into timely, applicable solutions for local communities.

Observing the lack of a place-responsive institutional commitment or strategy, which often frustrated the efforts of engaged researchers, Dostilio's work has focused on developing support infrastructure responsive to the institution's place-based legacies and obligations, thereby enhancing both the university's societal impact and support for individual investigators and projects.

Tensions uncovered in the university's work to establish a place-based approach, said Dostilio, included

- community feelings of overresearch and exploitation;
- research projects that seem abstract and far from offering immediately impactful solutions;
- projects disconnected from institution-level commitments and strategies;
- a primary focus on principal investigators, along with a lack of effort to develop local research staff into engagement professionals; and
- rigid institutional policies and practices, such as payment terms.

Dostilio noted that the university has since established infrastructure approaches to address the challenges, including

- long-term neighborhood commitments, such as the Neighborhood Commitments Initiative;[14]

---

[14] See https://www.community.pitt.edu/neighborhood-commitments

30 BUILDING INSTITUTIONAL CAPACITY FOR ENGAGED RESEARCH

- large-scale research studies, such as the Pittsburgh Study;[15]
- training and certifications for engagement professionals to develop needed competencies; and
- improved payment and contracting practices.

She invited further discussion about the ongoing tension around creating the job types, internal funding sources, convening functions, and other supports needed to enable faculty to be immediately responsive to community questions that are time-bound, urgent, and local.

Three Concepts for Infrastructure Change: Challenging Norms, Organizing, and Operationalizing

Noting that infrastructure change is a complex process, Adam Parris, director of climate resilience and senior consultant and environmental expert at ICF, said, "I think transformative change in the field of research will come in the form of [both] new institutions *and* change within institutions, and [from] large shifts *and* incremental improvements," rather than in one or the other. Gleaned from his diverse career spanning government, academia, and the private sector, Parris's philosophy of change is structured around three key concepts—namely, challenging existing norms, organizing, and operationalizing:

1. *Challenging norms*: Parris questioned the implicit assumption that research inherently helps people, advocating instead for a model of reciprocal knowledge exchange. A report on the topic of climate change,[16] based on his work with environmental justice leaders in New York City, outlines critical principles of knowledge exchange and provides five pathways to overhaul New York's environment for engaged research. The work repeatedly raised the question of what researchers are providing to communities in return for what they are asking from those communities, Parris said, which helped to embed the norm of reciprocity into his group's engaged research infrastructure. "Too often we ask for a lot in return for a little," he said.

2. *Organizing*: Parris emphasized the need to structure partnerships around shared, actionable outcomes, going beyond co-produced knowledge. Engaged research is part of a large web of actors, who play a role in these outcomes. Establishing the needed infrastructure

---

[15] See https://www.pediatrics.pitt.edu/centers-institutes/pittsburgh-study

[16] NYC Mayor's Office of Climate & Environmental Justice. (2022). *State of climate knowledge 2022: Workshop summary report.* City of New York. https://climate.cityofnewyork.us/wp-content/uploads/2022/04/2022_CKE_Report_10.25.22.pdf

TABLE 4-1 Core Competencies for Engaged Researchers

Area of Competency	Action Needed
Politics	Become more aware of public values and politics of science, including [their] role in decision making.
Social Capital	Build social ties and have fun.
Collaboration	Cultivate authentic relationships through transparency and self-awareness.
Communication/Exchange	Learn to communicate effectively and directly with and to diverse audiences.
Context	Develop ability to align different types of science and interaction with problem solving and decision making.
Evaluation	Design projects, programs, or activities with continual learning in mind.

SOURCE: Workshop presentation by Adam Parris.

requires understanding the interconnected nature of government, community, and academic roles, he explained, which ultimately drive policy and funding decisions. Organizing engaged research projects to promote shared accountability to research outcomes among this web of actors can enhance power sharing, he said.

3. *Operationalizing*: Parris underscored the need to empower researchers at all levels of their careers with "simple but routine" tools and core competencies for engaged research, including social and emotional skills, an awareness of the politics of science, the importance of social capital, and collaboration and communication skills. Table 4-1 provides a list of these core competencies.

Addressing Pain Points

Following the presentations, panelists discussed their approaches and models for streamlining infrastructure-related "pain points" that currently undermine engaged research.

- *Addressing communities' feelings of being overresearched*: Dostilio elaborated on the Neighborhood Commitments Initiative at the University of Pittsburgh, which was established to address communities' feelings of being overresearched. This initiative, supported by substantial facilities and institutional funding, involves long-term commitments between the university and key Pittsburgh neighborhoods to foster coherent, sustained community engagement. The initiative has provided "an exceptional space for people to feel connected to an anchoring strategy [. . .] and I think the coherency that's been created has been remarkable," she said.

- *Establishing innovative funding sources*: Parris noted that tensions around funding could be addressed by establishing new sources of revenue for universities that are aligned with the needs of local communities. Beyond tuition and indirect costs on funded research, Parris suggested innovative mechanisms, including allocating a small percentage of public utility revenues, with joint oversight, to support place-based engaged research, and using crowdfunding techniques.
- *Providing supportive data*: Providing supportive data to mid-level leaders who are attempting to advance engaged research could help them to demonstrate the value of this work to their leadership, Adsul said. She noted that such data can be generated using a mixed-methods approach that includes community voices, and she pointed to her team's creation of understandable data summaries, which can be leveraged with top officials to garner resources and support for community-engaged work.

Competencies and Capacity for Researchers

Susan Renoe, planning committee chair and associate vice chancellor at the University of Missouri, asked panelists about the integration of competencies into onboarding and capacity building, both in institutions and with community partners. Dostilio stated that competencies are considered in onboarding and professional development at the University of Pittsburgh, both for engagement staff and other university personnel with community engagement responsibilities. The university also offers an "engagement fundamentals competency certificate" for new team members, an approach that is not used with community-based partners because, often, "they are teaching us," she said. She also noted that the Community Involvement in Research Training and Implementation Certification[17] at the University of Illinois Chicago and the Community Partner Research Ethics Training[18] at the University of Pittsburgh are examples of accessible training for community-based practitioners, which allow community practitioners to be viewed as co-principal investigators in institutional review board systems.

Dostilio also highlighted the nationally validated competency model for engagement professionals that she uses at the University of Pittsburgh, which helps to build the necessary skills for supporting long-term partnerships and engaged research.

---

[17] See https://www.cctst.org/cirtification

[18] See https://ctsi.pitt.edu/education-training/community-partners-research-ethics-training/

Capacity Building for Communities

The panel discussion also addressed building capacity for or with local organizations to support their engagement with research. Parris shared his experience with the Cycles of Resilience project in New York City,[19] which included participatory budgeting processes. In this project, his role as a researcher from the City University of New York was not to lead the project but rather to work with the community to map the locations of particular challenges it faced (e.g., flooding) and formulate project ideas that it could then continue. This process enabled communities to be better equipped to advocate with the City of New York and to engage in participatory budgeting processes of the city.

One participant noted that it can be challenging to establish the boundaries between a research institution and a community organization—for example, when a community organization might want a researcher to act on its behalf. Parris noted that in his work in New York, his team established a boundary of clarifying policy choices and bolstering those choices with evidence, while the community determined the choices it advocated.

Communication and Knowledge Exchange

A workshop participant asked the panel whether particular modes of communication can best support bidirectional engagement between communities and researchers. Panelists responded with several key points:

- Understanding the specific communication preferences in each partnership is critical, noted Adsul.
- Creating a unified institutional point of contact for community members (e.g., community engagement offices), aligned with the institution's engagement-related mission, can ease communication at the institutional level, said Adsul. Parris mentioned that, while rare, some government agencies have community engagement offices in their planning departments.
- Boundary setting is a critical aspect of effective communication, noted Parris, advising that all stakeholders should strive to "be direct and authentic; set expectations up front and just be honest about what you can and can't accomplish."
- Networks for knowledge exchange between scientists, institutions, and communities can be valuable resources, noted both Dostilio and Adsul, and they offered three examples: the Advancing

---

[19] See https://srijb.org/cycles/#:~:text=The%20Cycles%20model%20is%20a,to%20turn%20ideas%20into%20action

Research Impact in Society,[20] the Community-Campus Partnerships for Health,[21] and the Community Engagement Alliance at the National Institutes of Health.[22]

COMMON THEMES AND GAPS

Panelists and attendees shared their observations and questions around prevailing themes that arose during discussions about key tensions and the gaps that remain in addressing these tensions to expand institutional capacity for engaged research.

Understanding Existing Structures

KerryAnn O'Meara, vice president for academic affairs, provost, and dean at Teachers College, Columbia University, shared thoughts on the need to understand the historical purposes of institutional structures before attempting to change them. She used the analogy of walking into a messy closet, where initial impressions of disorganization might conceal underlying systems that serve specific purposes. For example, when structures are changed, autonomous projects that have flourished without institutional oversight might require integration into broader university initiatives without stifling their innovative potential, O'Meara said. She emphasized the delicate balance between maintaining beneficial autonomous initiatives and addressing power issues or other structures that hinder progress. By recognizing the "origin stories" and current functions of existing structures, institutions can make informed decisions in such situations, added Elyse Aurbach, planning committee member and director for public engagement and research impacts at the University of Michigan.

Financial Barriers, Funding, and Risk

A request for a show of hands about participants' experience of money-related tensions in engaged research indicated that most participants had experienced such barriers. Aurbach emphasized that money is an expression of power, necessitating a careful, mindful approach to the logistics around both large and small financial commitments. As noted by a workshop participant, the complexities of funding flows have negative implications for both community partners and researchers. Examples include community partners who were expected to work for extended periods without

---

[20] See researchinsociety.org
[21] See https://ccphealth.org/
[22] See https://ceal.nih.gov/

receiving promised financial support or researchers who wanted to divert funds directly to community partners but might receive less credit for their work by doing so.

On the researcher side, one participant raised the common practice of using indirect costs to support basic science labs, noting that similar financial support is often not extended to engaged researchers. A participant suggested that some financial challenges could be addressed by submitting incentive payments and other community engagement costs as direct costs, rather than as indirect costs, in grant proposals, and urged funders to recognize these costs as essential components of research projects. A participant pointed out that grant reviewers may not understand the need for community compensation or other costs of engaged research, necessitating defined, uniform criteria as well as training for review panels, peer reviewers, and publishers.

Emily Ozer, planning committee member and clinical and community psychologist and professor of public health and faculty liaison to the executive vice chancellor and provost for public scholarship and engagement at UC, Berkeley, raised the issue of institutional risk tolerance, which is often closely tied to funding decisions, and its impact on community partnerships. Overly conservative views on risk could hinder the development of effective and timely community-engaged research, Ozer pointed out. She advocated for a broader understanding of institutional policies and legal frameworks to support flexible and responsive financial arrangements, suggesting that influential funders could play a pivotal role in pushing institutions to adopt supportive policies for partnered work.

On the community side, partnerships need to be sustained and financially supported, particularly between grant cycles, to ensure that community partners continue to be compensated, one participant said, pointing out that gaps in funding are particularly problematic for small, community-based organizations that juggle multiple roles and responsibilities. Another participant proposed simplifying the funding process and increasing its equitability by allowing community partners to receive funds directly from funders rather than through institutions.

Using Data and Shared Language

Documenting faculty support through surveys can provide a data-driven approach to advocating for engaged research, said Rich Carter, professor of chemistry at Oregon State University and faculty lead of Promotion & Tenure—Innovation & Entrepreneurship. In his experience, surveys have provided concrete data that can be used to influence mid-level administrators and build a case for institutional support for engaged work. Involving faculty from various departments and ranks in defining key survey terms and concepts helped his team create an inclusive, representative understanding of engaged scholarship, Carter said. This approach both built familiarity with important terminology and gathered essential data to support advocacy efforts.

Building on Carter's points, a participant emphasized the need for clarity and common terminology across differing types of engagement work. She noted the importance of distinguishing between various forms of engagement, such as community engagement and policy engagement. There is a common lack of understanding and recognition of methods and best practices, even within the engagement field, which can lead to misconceptions and undervaluation of certain approaches, she said. Developing a shared language about the components of good practice in each type of engagement, she suggested, could both assist efforts to recognize and support diverse forms of impactful work and improve evaluation and recognition of engagement activities in tenure and promotion processes.

Reflective Practices and Global Perspectives

Institutions often suffer from a gap in honest self-reflection, said Marisol Morales, executive director of the Carnegie Elective Classifications and assistant vice president at the American Council on Education, often due to a preoccupation with rankings and reputation. Reflecting on their histories of harm and considering ways to address these issues could break down institutional barriers to community participation, she said. Morales expressed optimism, stating, "We built this. We can change it. And so, I'm hoping that through these conversations we can get to that place of dismantling the things that haven't worked and building things that will." She noted that some international universities, including those in Australia, Canada, and South Africa, have made significant strides in reflectively redressing harms and could thus serve as models for U.S. institutions.

A workshop participant expanded on Morales's points about universities being reflective. He discussed ongoing efforts in South African higher education to "decolonize" knowledge and recognize diverse ways of knowing—an approach that challenges traditional notions of valid, legitimate knowledge and calls for an inclusive understanding that values contributions from all partners. The participant's comments, Aurbach pointed out, underscore the need for U.S. institutions to broaden their perspectives and incorporate diverse epistemologies into their research practices. She referenced the Center for Braiding Indigenous Knowledges and Science project,[23] funded by the National Science Foundation, which explores ethically combining Western philosophies around academic research and knowledge with Indigenous ways of knowing, to address urgent, interconnected challenges.

---

[23] See https://www.umass.edu/gateway/research/indigenous-knowledges

Leveraging Cooperative Extension Systems

Cooperative extension systems have a long history of working closely with communities and could provide valuable insights and models for other institutions, noted a workshop participant. Since many of the workshop conversations mirror issues faced by extension systems, understanding how these systems operate could help universities develop more effective strategies for community engagement, one participant stated: "A whole body of practitioners within academia that maybe have been struggling with some of these issues since the land-grant university system was put together might have really useful contributions." Aurbach mentioned her recent experience learning about cooperative extensions and pointed out that some university systems, like the University of Missouri, do not separate extension into specific parts of the university and thus can engage broadly to understand community priorities.

Focus on Generating Solutions: Ideas from Workshop Participants

Workshop participants also offered their own insights about the tensions they were experiencing in their own contexts, and shared innovations and promising approaches for addressing those tensions organized into the categories depicted in Box 3-1. Participants were also invited to share other ideas that may not have been captured in their categories or in the presentations. After this idea-generating activity, planning committee members identified themes among the ideas that participants shared. These categories and participant ideas are available on the project website.[24]

---

[24] See https://www.nationalacademies.org/event/42782_06-2024_building-institutional-capacity-for-engaged-research-a-workshop#sectionEventMaterials

5

Aligning Mission and Incentives: Valuing and Prioritizing Engaged Research

Building capacity for engaged research can involve combining the diverse and often conflicting missions and incentives of various actors and sectors. A panel discussion brought together five leaders from several sectors to discuss this issue. Cheryl Boyce, assistant director for re-engineering the research enterprise at the National Institutes of Health (NIH), offered perspectives on how the priorities of a large funder can shape approaches to engaged research. Rich Carter, professor of chemistry at Oregon State University (OSU) and faculty lead of Promotion & Tenure – Innovation & Entrepreneurship (PTIE),[1] described insights from PTIE on aligning mission and incentives. KerryAnn O'Meara, vice president for academic affairs, provost, and dean at Teachers College, Columbia University, shared views on institutional change as a university leader. Marisol Morales, executive director of the Carnegie Elective Classifications and assistant vice president at the American Council on Education, offered insights from her vantage point at an accrediting organization. Toby Smith, senior vice president for government relations and public policy at the Association of American Universities (AAU), provided his views from the vantage point of a large national association of academic institutions. Panelists discussed key topics related to valuing and prioritizing engaged research, including the role of engaged research in institutional excellence, community demand for engaged research, promotion and tenure considerations, strategies for incentivizing engaged research at scale, and methods for measuring its impact.

---

[1] See https://ptie.org/

QUALITIES OF AN EXCELLENT INSTITUTION

Panelists began by sharing their perspectives on what it means to be an excellent research institution in a culture that values engaged research. Three key qualities emerged from the discussions: prioritizing community involvement, innovative promotion and tenure processes, and agility, adaptability, and responsiveness.

Prioritizing Community Involvement

Prioritizing community involvement is an important component of institutional excellence in engaged research, noted two panelists. Boyce noted that the NIH Common Fund prioritizes transformation and has a unique vantage point in that research institutions are partners in NIH's mission of enhancing health, lengthening life, and reducing illness and disability through excellent science. She emphasized that one of the best models for scientific excellence is the prioritization of community involvement throughout the entire research process. This approach requires participating institutions to allocate sufficient resources, including personnel, financial support, and, importantly, time to support community engagement. By integrating these aspects into their frameworks, Boyce stated, research institutions that work with NIH can foster mutually beneficial relationships and advance the mission of engaged research.

Carter explained that prioritizing community engagement can also help institutions recruit and train the next generation of scholars and entrepreneurs, noting that such actions also align with students' desires for societal impact.

Innovative Promotion and Tenure Processes

Several panelists emphasized the importance of reflecting what excellence means through reformed promotion and tenure processes to incentivize and reward engaged research. Smith said the faculty at many of the 71 AAU are ingrained with a "cookie-cutter" view of excellence based on research, publications, and grant funding. However, to achieve excellence in the four missions established for AAU universities (i.e., science, teaching, service, and economic development), institutions need to extend beyond those traditional metrics to value diverse faculty contributions. He argued that true excellence needs to be assessed holistically at the departmental level, rather than at the individual faculty level, to recognize the varied roles faculty play—from traditional research to community engagement and entrepreneurship. The four missions reflect the need for engaged work: "If we are not seen as a public good, and we're only seen as valuing the faculty working at our institutions or the students who attend them, we've got a problem. And right now, we have a problem, and we've got to address it," Smith said.

O'Meara echoed the need to move away from cookie-cutter evaluation approaches, with the metaphor used by Sapna Cheryan of the University of Washington of fitting through a "cardboard cutout" to describe how existing frameworks are often ill-suited to the unique impacts of engaged work. Redefining hiring, promotion, tenure, retention, and awards processes to foster an environment in which all forms of scholarship are valued involves "scripting and educating and appropriately making sure that the evaluation that's happening for folks in their different lanes is appropriate to the context within which they are working," she stated.

Carter noted that the consensus recommendations for evaluating faculty based on innovation and entrepreneurship also apply to evaluating community-engaged work. Developed through engagement with 70 universities and 12 stakeholder organizations, the PTIE consensus process yielded four recommendations: (a) linking faculty evaluations with the values, goals, and priorities of the university; (b) developing the metrics to evaluate in keeping with those values, goals, and priorities; (c) recognizing that innovation, entrepreneurship, or community-engaged work happens in areas of faculty work beyond research; and (d) addressing the implicit bias that happens in the evaluation process.

"Promotion and tenure sit at the fulcrum of change on a campus," said Carter. While fair and transparent evaluation processes foster excellent research institutions that value engaged scholarship, promotion and tenure are just "one of the many levers," he pointed out. "If you're not thinking about this when you're hiring, if you're not thinking about this at annual evaluations, if you're not thinking about this in how you do a position description, how you assign space [and] how you assign resources, the whole house of cards falls apart." While the exact definition of an excellent university will vary across institutions, he said, valuing a diverse ecosystem of faculty contributions, aligned with university values and goals, is a key component.

Agility, Adaptability, and Responsiveness

The qualities institutions exhibited during the COVID-19 pandemic are illustrative of excellent research institutions, stated Morales—namely, agility, adaptability, and responsiveness to changing community needs. To instill such qualities, institutions need courageous leaders at all levels, to push against the artificial constraints of traditional rankings and metrics. Echoing Carter's comments, Morales further called for institutions to hire and train employees based on institutional values and to ensure evaluators at all levels

42   BUILDING INSTITUTIONAL CAPACITY FOR ENGAGED RESEARCH

understand and implement these values. The true measure of excellence, she said, is represented by tangible improvements in communities, such as policy changes, poverty reduction, and addressing income disparities.

LESSONS FROM THE NATIONAL INSTITUTES OF HEALTH MODELS FOR FUNDING COMMUNITIES DIRECTLY

Boyce discussed her insights from NIH's direct funding to communities and the capacity-building needs of community organizations. She explained that recent strategic efforts have galvanized NIH's long-standing history of community funding. For example, during the COVID-19 pandemic, initiatives like the Community Engagement Alliance[2] and RADx-UP[3] emerged to involve communities directly in health interventions, demonstrating the importance of flexible and rapid responses. Community feedback revealed a need for genuine co-creation and equitable, community-driven partnerships in which communities are funded directly, not paid as subcontractors, said Boyce. This need led NIH to look to models, such as Native American Research Centers for Health,[4] for new ways to fund community organizations. Subsequently for Community Partnerships to Advance Science for Society,[5] NIH paid communities directly for the first time, through its Other Transactional Authority awards.[6] The unprecedented response to this new funding model indicated community organizations' readiness and enthusiasm. Boyce noted that phased awards and planning time can ensure sustainable, effective interventions that communities want and need, ultimately advancing public health through inclusive, engaged research practices.

Boyce emphasized that NIH funding serves as a significant incentive for engaged research. She noted an array of funding mechanisms designed to incentivize diverse and impactful research approaches, including collaborative agreements, phased awards, other transaction awards, and small business mechanisms. Tailoring the language of announcements to select for certain types of applications can serve as an additional type of incentive, Boyce noted. She also pointed out the recent Communities Advancing Research Equity

---

[2] See https://ceal.nih.gov/

[3] See https://radx-up.org/

[4] National Institute of General Medical Sciences. (2024). *Native American Research Centers for Health (NARCH)*. National Institutes of Health, U.S. Department of Health and Human Services. https://www.nigms.nih.gov/capacity-building/division-for-research-capacity-building/native-american-research-centers-for-health-(narch)

[5] See https://commonfund.nih.gov/compass

[6] See https://www.era.nih.gov/erahelp/ASSIST/Content/ASSIST_Help_Topics/OTA/OTA_About.htm#:~:text=An%20Other%20Transaction%20(OT)%20is,terms%20and%20conditions%20of%20award

ALIGNING MISSION AND INCENTIVES   *43*

for Health™ initiative,[7] which aims to build trust and relationships in the primary care setting. To sum up the incentive for engaged research provided by NIH, she concluded, "The incentive is funding, but it's the incentive for funding that makes sense based on what we know in science [and] what we know about working with communities that really leads to a better outcome. We want sustainable interventions that work [and] really improve health."

CHANGING EVALUATION:
LEVERAGING DISCRETIONARY MOMENTS

O'Meara highlighted the main types of steps institutions are using to address the disincentivizing of engaged scholarship in promotion and tenure evaluations. Both systemic change and incremental steps are required to improve evaluative spaces, she emphasized, noting that it is a work in progress— "we are building the plane as we fly it." Achieving systemic change requires many discretionary "micro moments" or opportunities for leaders to make impactful decisions that can provide needed support or resources outside of formal processes, along the trajectory, O'Meara noted. She categorized these changes in three types of discretion that people may already have within their existing authority at their institutions: leveraging, checking, and restructuring.

1. *Leveraging discretion*: Small changes, or "micro moments," can reorient the way people view engaged research, such as updated job descriptions that emphasize the value of engaged scholarship, and scripts in promotion letter requests emphasizing an institution's support of engaged research. Even the organization of a curriculum vitae can leverage a viewer's discretion to see engaged work differently, she said, pointing out an example in which diversity, equity, and inclusion work was weighted more heavily when it was consolidated in one part of a curriculum vitae rather than throughout teaching, research, and service sections.
2. *Checking discretion*: This practice involves ensuring that important practices are happening, O'Meara explained. "We're going to [. . .] check because we're not quite sure the plane is flying right and this person's getting a fair deal." Such actions could include ensuring that promotion and tenure committee members are knowledgeable about interdisciplinary work or ensuring that an institution has engaged scholars in its applicant pool.
3. *Restructuring discretion*: Large-scale changes that involve creating new faculty roles or even entire institutions that embed a novel set of rules can leverage equity and support for engaged scholarship.

---

[7] See https://commonfund.nih.gov/clinical-research-primary-care

BUILDING CAPACITY FOR INNOVATION
AND ENTREPRENEURSHIP

Carter explained that the existing capacity of a university to engage with industry can be leveraged in its interactions with private-sector organizations—some capacities can serve both innovation and community engagement needs. Carter emphasized three commonalities between innovation/ entrepreneurship and engaged research:

1. Faculty and students need proper training in these areas.
2. Seed funding is critical for catalyzing new ideas in both entrepreneurship and community-engaged work.
3. Creating opportunities for faculty—particularly junior faculty—to network with industry or community partners can help them to get started.

Echoing other panelists, Carter stressed the need for institutions to develop policies and procedures that value nontraditional academic outputs, such as innovation/entrepreneurship and engaged research. For example, embedding awards and incentives throughout the academic ecosystem can sustain researchers' efforts in these areas, ensuring that the culture of engagement persists regardless of changes in senior administration, he said.

THE ROLE OF PROFESSIONAL ORGANIZATION
REQUIREMENTS IN ENCOURAGING ENGAGED RESEARCH

Two panelists from professional organizations—the American Council on Education, which helps to administer the Carnegie Elective Classifications, including the Carnegie Elective Classification for Community Engagement, and AAU—discussed their perspectives on valuing engaged research and highlighted ways that their organizations can encourage universities in this regard.

Carnegie Elective Classification

Morales explained how the Carnegie Elective Classification for Community Engagement both encourages innovation and improvement in the core academic functions of higher education and builds capacity for engaged research. The classification serves as a recognition and accountability measure, she explained, but at the same time it promotes continuous improvement and institutional transformation. She noted that "the process is the prize," explaining that recognition is not the most important aspect of the classification—by requiring institutions to reflect on their practices and policies, the classification process drives them to implement needed changes.

The classification continues to evolve based on campus trends, best practices, and a community partner survey, Morales said. For example, she pointed out the inclusion of a new section on civic life and learning in the 2026 cycle, with questions about voter participation rates and free speech policies. "The things that need to show up, we try to make them show up," she said. She also noted the recent implementation of individualized feedback reports, which provide campuses with specific, actionable insights for enhancing engagement efforts.

Morales described initial data from reclassification applications—namely, explicit language around tenure and promotion policies—indicating that the Carnegie Classification process incentivizes institutions to make concrete progress toward valuing engaged research. She invited collaboration to further refine their metrics and leverage their extensive data to understand trends and best practices for incentivizing engaged research in higher education.

The Role of the Association of American Universities in Promoting Engaged Research

Smith explored the unique role of AAU in both incentivizing and disincentivizing engaged research. Beginning with disincentives, Smith noted that research remains a central focus in AAU evaluations and that traditional evaluation metrics are deeply ingrained in academic culture and often hinder change. However, in terms of incentives, he noted that there is a growing recognition within AAU of the need to evaluate universities on a broader set of metrics, including community engagement.

While institutional leaders might advocate for change, true transformation requires grassroots support from faculty, Smith said. To illustrate such a grassroots approach, he used the example of teaching excellence—one pillar of excellence supported by AAU. The traditional metric used to evaluate teaching excellence, namely teacher evaluations, is widely believed to be ineffective. Institutional leadership could begin to change this deeply ingrained practice by facilitating departmental discussions about alternative teaching evaluation methods, including diverse artifacts of excellence, such as syllabi and teaching philosophies. New strategies could then be incorporated into evaluation practices and, along with structural changes, including altering promotion and tenure committees and establishing a vice chair for undergraduate teaching, could ultimately shift a department's emphasis from research to teaching, Smith suggested.

He also pointed out that other professional societies, funding agencies, and publication standards could provide additional incentives for change by broadening their criteria for excellence to recognize and support engaged research.

INVESTMENTS FOR SUSTAINABLE ENGAGED RESEARCH

The final topic of the panel discussion focused on investments necessary for sustaining engaged research over time. In a recent vision and action plan process at Teachers College, during which engaged scholars were asked what they needed to succeed, several replied "cover," or institutional support, O'Meara reported. For example, faculty need their leaders and faculty colleagues to understand that innovative partnership work takes time and is complex. It may have an effect on the timing and number of publications or grants, require new kinds of memoranda of understanding and agreements with partner organizations, and/or support for new kinds of field-based teaching. This need illustrates the importance of investing in institutional structures and processes that can provide that type of institutional support for doing research in new ways, she said.

Carter added that hiring faculty is a critical opportunity to create a more inclusive campus and that search committees need to be built deliberately to foster inclusivity and change. "If you're expecting a department to think of new things and to do new things, building a committee made up of the old things is not very likely to generate the new things," he said. He pointed out OSU's Search Advocate Program,[8] which helps ensure diverse and innovative hiring practices by providing tools and interventions to address biases.

NIH has a strong history of supporting faculty through various career-spanning awards and programs aimed at building inclusive excellence, Boyce added. She expressed interest in using data to evaluate how a climate of inclusivity might relate to research funding and innovation, and she noted the usefulness of metrics presented during the workshop for guiding resource-allocation decisions that could help institutions achieve engaged research goals.

DISCUSSION

To follow up, the panelists and other workshop participants discussed various aspects of aligning missions and incentives to value and prioritize engaged research, including time constraints and sustainability, and the role of legislation.

Time Constraints

The panel discussed a number of challenges that time poses to the feasibility and sustainability of engaged research, including the long time frames sometimes needed to see an impact, the amount of time it takes to

---

[8] See https://searchadvocate.oregonstate.edu/

build relationships and the mismatch with the lengths of grants and funding cycles, and the time-consuming nature of the work.

Smith reiterated the challenge of limited faculty time, noting, "If you expect every faculty member to do everything we want them to do, they will never be able to do it."

Several suggestions were made for developing relationships and achieving impact despite time constraints:

- Create a diverse faculty with varied skill sets to achieve comprehensive excellence (Smith).
- Develop frameworks that incorporate sufficient time for relationship-building and planning activities (Morales).
- Establish flexible tenure and evaluation models and alternative timelines for meeting criteria in teaching, research, and service to address time-related challenges in faculty evaluations (O'Meara).
- Provide institutional financial support to sustain key programs and relationships with communities beyond the traditional funding period, such as NIH's 10-year Community Partnerships to Advance Science for Society program, which builds in time for comprehensive evaluation, impact assessment, and sustainability (Smith and Boyce).

Improving Measurement of Engaged Research

Establishing metrics is one of the most tension-filled aspects of evaluating engaged research, said Carter. Moving beyond traditional conversion factors to a broad collection of metrics, such as those established by PTIE,[9] can better value individuals throughout the life-cycle of their work. "There is no conversion factor. We should not be boiled down to a number. We should not be boiled down to some ratio. It's about a narrative thesis of impact," Carter stated. Boyce and O'Meara echoed the idea that evaluation metrics need to capture discovery, innovation, and overall impact.

Boyce also suggested that strong metrics can both improve outcomes and document the opportunities of existing programs. O'Meara added that engaged scholars need to be given the latitude to define their objectives and outcomes. She shared an example of a scholar who influenced state policy to provide subsidies to underresourced mothers, highlighting the need for evaluation metrics that measure diverse impacts, such as policy changes and community health improvements. Morales added that

---

[9] See https://ir.library.oregonstate.edu/concern/defaults/jw827k251

engaged scholars and community partners require considerable time to work together to determine "what success looks like" for a project.

Sustainability

Given the long time frame of community-engaged research, a follow-up question addressed the sustainability of programs across leadership changes at various levels. In response, panelists brought forth several relevant points.

- Data are key in proving the efficacy and impact of community-engaged scholarship to successive leaders, ensuring continuity of support (Boyce).
- Embedding engaged research throughout an institution's mission statement, strategic plan, accreditation documents, and other accountability measures can promote sustainability. "So, it doesn't matter who's in charge. Whoever comes to be president is already walking into a place that they know believes in this. And it's part of their ethos" (Morales).
- Sustainability can also be driven by community engagement—community stakeholders can take ownership of programs and advocate for their continuation (Smith).

The Role of Legislation

Susan Renoe, planning committee chair and associate vice chancellor at the University of Missouri, asked Smith whether legislation like the CHIPS and Science Act[10] could help to align missions and incentives to bolster engaged research, akin to the Bayh-Dole Act for university technology transfer. Smith expressed skepticism, noting the lack of funding for the new TIP directorate and emphasizing the ongoing challenges in achieving knowledge exchange beyond patents and licenses. Given the current funding realities, Smith stressed the need to advocate for National Science Foundation (NSF) funding to support technological innovation. Carter reminded the audience that challenges related to the Bayh-Dole Act still exist 44 years after its implementation, suggesting that legislative solutions alone are insufficient.

INSIGHTS FROM KEY LEADERS

The workshop also featured reflections from two institutional leaders. Neeli Bendapudi, president of Penn State University, offered her views on

---

[10] CHIPS and Science Act, Pub. Law No. 117-167, 136 Stat. 1366 (2022). https://www.congress.gov/bill/117th-congress/house-bill/4346

the strategic opportunities for university leaders. Erwin Gianchandani, the NSF assistant director of the Directorate for Technology, Innovation and Partnerships (TIP), reflected on the challenges and opportunities for advancing engaged research within academia.

To address the perennial challenge of making real change in academia toward prioritizing public impact research—a goal that has been pursued for decades without consistent success—Bendapudi introduced the nascent Presidents and Chancellors Council on Public Impact Research. This group, which met for the first time in the days before the workshop for initial conversations, was organized by Bendapudi, Angela Bednarek of The Pew Charitable Trusts, and the Transforming Evidence Funders Network, a group led by Bednarek that aims to create a meta-network of funders, university presidents, and government agencies that "has stickiness to it" and can make a substantial and lasting impact.

Bendapudi articulated three main reasons that the current moment is crucial for advancing public impact research. First, questioning the value of higher education is becoming more widespread, and steps are required to address this existential threat. Higher education institutions need to increase efforts to effectively communicate their worth and relevance, she noted. Second, Bendapudi expressed deep concern over the declining trust in expertise and science, which she believes poses a threat to democracy itself. The evolving nature of scientific knowledge, which can contribute to lack of public trust, is not a deficit, she noted, but is an intrinsic characteristic of the scientific method. Last, she highlighted the relatively short tenure of university leaders, which makes it imperative to build systemic, rather than individual, solutions.

In her role as president of Penn State, Bendapudi sees a unique opportunity to champion public impact research. She described Penn State's distinctive structure, with 24 campuses across Pennsylvania, many of which serve majority-minority and first-generation students. This diverse and extensive network provides a fertile ground for engaging in meaningful public impact research. Bendapudi noted that today's students care deeply about such research and that involving them can enhance their engagement and persistence in higher education. She emphasized that expertise is not enough—academic institutions need to be seen as both competent *and* well-intentioned to build and maintain trust and effectively engage communities. She called for greater involvement of professional organizations in valuing engaged research. While public impact research should not detract from basic research, it is critical that engaged research involve genuine knowledge creation, not merely service, she said.

To conclude, she used the analogy of a sports team to call for a cultural shift that appreciates the varied contributions of faculty members, which collectively can make universities a "triple threat"—excelling in research, teaching, and service.

Gianchandani provided a complementary view by discussing NSF's evolving role in driving use-inspired, impact-driven research through strategic partnerships and capacity building. While NSF is well known for its long history of supporting basic, foundational science and engineering, it is less known for its focus on use-inspired, impact-driven research, he said. The TIP directorate aims to accelerate the process of foundational research to impact by fostering collaboration and addressing societal, economic, and national challenges. This focus on use-inspired, impact-driven science complements—and does not distract from—NSF support of foundational work, he explained.

NSF has been committed to engaged research and researcher-participant partnerships for many years, said Gianchandani. "We just don't talk about it as much at NSF and, frankly, we just don't invest as much in it as we invest on the foundational side of the house." Programs like Smart and Connected Communities[11] and the Civic Innovation Challenge[12] were early efforts to bridge research with practical community needs. To accomplish TIP's mission of accelerating research to impact and broadening participation, Gianchandani noted the directorate's two-fold focus: growing the capacity of institutions, including emerging and minority-serving institutions, to participate in engaged work; and establishing a balanced approach within NSF between foundational science and use-inspired research. Some NSF programs aim to work collaboratively with institutions to address their unique challenges and maximize their potential of success in NSF funding competitions, including Enabling Partnerships to Increase Innovation Capacity[13] and Accelerating Research Translation.[14]

The time is ripe, Gianchandani said, for advancing impactful research through collaborative, cross-sectoral efforts. Many students today are motivated by a desire to create a positive and lasting impact on society. These students believe in science and engineering as tools for societal transformation and are eager to tackle real-world challenges. He urged immediate action to capitalize on the motivation of students toward societally transformative work, framing the current moment as a generational opportunity to advance impactful research.

---

[11] See https://new.nsf.gov/funding/opportunities/scc-smart-connected-communities

[12] See https://new.nsf.gov/funding/opportunities/civic-civic-innovation-challenge

[13] See https://new.nsf.gov/funding/opportunities/enabling-partnerships-increase-innovation-capacity

[14] See https://new.nsf.gov/funding/opportunities/accelerating-research-translation-art

6

Valuing Diverse Forms of Expertise

Byron White, planning committee member and associate provost for urban research and community engagement at the University of North Carolina (UNC) at Charlotte, began his remarks by noting that much of the distribution of power and shared authority is tied to the perception of where expertise resides, and the common belief is that academic institutions hold the expertise. While many engaged researchers have moved beyond the idea of viewing communities as simply research subjects, communities are still commonly viewed through a deficit lens—as needy and reliant on institutional expertise, he stated. True co-production requires a perspective shift that values community skills and expertise on par with those of researchers, worthy of comparable levels of power and authority. He illustrated this shift by describing a project at Cleveland State University designed to address the high rate of diabetes in a predominantly Black neighborhood. While the traditional, deficit-oriented approach viewed the community as in need of training in diabetes care, recognizing residents' extensive experiences in managing diabetes reoriented researchers to see community members as highly skilled and capable trainers rather than "needy" recipients of training. "So, rather than asking community organizations to enlist trainees, it might be to identify the best trainers," he explained.

Panelists shared their experiences and insights on building partnerships that genuinely integrate and value diverse forms of expertise.

SHIFTING DYNAMICS OF EXPERTISE IN
RESEARCH-PRACTICE PARTNERSHIPS

William Penuel, distinguished professor of learning sciences and human development at the University of Colorado Boulder, described shifts in the dynamics of power and expertise that he has experienced through his collaborative work with Denver Public Schools over the past 17 years, primarily focused on supporting standards implementation through curriculum and curriculum-linked professional learning. These activities are key systems-level leverage points for equity-oriented change, Penuel explained. In the past several years, the partnership has focused on co-design of curriculum. Co-design, a core practice in his research-practice partnerships, intrinsically involves valuing practitioners' expertise, he said. "Often researchers come to me who are interested in partnerships, but they have an intervention already developed. And they want other people just to use it, and then they want to call that a partnership. And the question I ask, and I use this language, because this is how they think about it, [is] are you willing to have your intervention mangled? And if you are not, you are not ready for partnership. Because you don't yet value sufficiently the expertise of the people who are going to adapt and implement that." In a co-design model, teachers are scholars alongside the researchers, contributing directly to the insights of research.

To illustrate, Penuel described the development of the OpenSciEd[1] high school science curriculum, which aimed to provide more equitable classroom experiences for science, technology, engineering, and mathematics (STEM). In this project, teachers served as full-time members of the design team, not just as classroom implementers, and they also participated alongside researchers in interpreting data. By positioning teachers as experts, the team used teachers' first-hand experiences and insights in curriculum development. Careful facilitation created an environment in which practitioners' voices were genuinely valued and integrated, Penuel said.

Douglas Watkins, manager of K–12 science curriculum and instruction and Penuel's connection to teachers and administrators at Denver Public Schools, offered his perspectives on working in collaboration with Penuel and his team. He addressed the implementation of the curriculum project. The project was collaborative from the beginning, Watkins said, noting his involvement in identifying problems of practice and shaping the direction of the work. Although Watkins was initially skeptical about the value of the project, he changed his perspective 10 months later after spending 2 days experiencing the co-designed curriculum as a student. That experience convinced him of the curriculum's potential to provide more equitable

---

[1] See https://www.openscied.org/

VALUING DIVERSE FORMS OF EXPERTISE

STEM experiences in classrooms. From that moment on, Watkins said, he was "all in," and he focused on recruiting as many teachers as possible who could experience the same "light bulb click" and become leaders in promoting the new approach.

CENTERING COMMUNITY EXPERTISE
IN RESEARCH PARTNERSHIPS

Eboné Lockett, chief executive officer and principal consultant of Harvesting Humanity,[2] was asked to describe how she decides whether to participate in research partnerships. Lockett began by introducing herself: "I am the great granddaughter of migrant and immigrant farmers. I currently reside in Charlotte, North Carolina, because it was a return to finding out who I am and whose I am and who I'm responsible to and who I'm responsible for." Thus, her primary consideration, she explained, lies in ensuring research partnerships genuinely serve her community—namely, that they center and respect community members and honor their humanity. "Is this serving the people that I'm responsible to and who I'm responsible for? [. . .] That is my first lens, and that is the first measure."

Lockett also described the relationship-building process that proceeded any involvement with research. The first significant collaboration developed through a personal interaction with White. "You have to meet people at that human-to-human connection first. And then I shared all my degrees [. . .] all of the things that allowed me to be able to walk in my expertise as an academic, but also first and foremost, my expertise as a community member," she stated. Through the connection with White, Lockett was able to approach him for help in finding a research partner to enable the high school students from a local Title I school that she worked with to study the water quality in their school and community. White was able to facilitate a connection between Lockett and a researcher that led to a successful grant application in which Lockett and the researcher were co-principal investigators. The positive experience working in collaboration over the 2 years of that project led to meaningful experiences for Lockett's students, including presenting their research posters at a conference, which played a role in Lockett's openness to considering future research collaborations.

Ian Binns, associate professor at the Cato College of Education, UNC–Charlotte, and lead community engagement recruiter for the Computational Intelligence to Predict Health and Environmental Risks (CIPHER) Center, described his experience working collaboratively with Lockett on a proposal to address community environmental and health risks. He described how CIPHER navigates engagement with community partners and how

---

[2] See https://www.harvestinghumanity.com/

he convinces his peers of the value of such collaborations. In communicating with his multidisciplinary team of researchers, Binns stressed the importance of learning what the community needed in terms of predicting environmental or health risks. As he explained, "We can't approach communities and expect that they are just going to listen and do what we ask. That's not the way this works." Although scientists do "bring something to the table," they do not hold all the answers and need to approach partnership work as such, he said.

In sharing his experience meeting Lockett and approaching a potential partnership, Binns described how Lockett pushed him in their initial interactions. She helped him realize that his actions were not always reflecting humility, Binns explained. Echoing earlier panelists, Lockett said, "When researchers come to the community, it is often with the assumption that the expertise doesn't already reside in the community." However, she noted, community members, especially those who are most affected by the issues being studied, often have the capacity, degrees, and language to understand the problem, as well as valuable insights and experiences that can inform the research.

"It was an uncomfortable feeling during that first meeting with Eboné, but instead of turning and running, I chose to sit with it. I made sure that I sat there and listened and did not defend anything. I listened because I realized that's what I had to do," Binns said, noting that he subsequently adjusted his approach. He shared this experience with his team to emphasize that building genuine partnerships requires listening and the willingness to endure discomfort.

VALUING EXPERTISE AT SCALE

To illustrate how community expertise can be recognized "at scale" in broader contexts, Penuel elaborated on his work with Denver Public Schools. He explained that the initial National Science Foundation-funded inquiryHub[3] project involved co-designing a limited number of pilot units for a biology curriculum. Penuel recalled a pivotal moment when a school district administrator, recognizing the value of the product, requested the co-design of a complete curriculum, which the district funded. This deep investment into local work had a paradoxical effect, said Penuel, in that it facilitated broader adoption and scaling of the curriculum beyond his district. He said,

> And suddenly this paradox emerges that this careful local work is what enables work to scale. And this is not what we usually think. We think the way to make things work is to design for anywhere. But the paradoxes

---

[3] See https://www.colorado.edu/program/inquiryhub/

of scale for me are two things. One is that the way you make something scalable is to do deep local work so that it can work some place first, and then remember that it's relationships all the way down in the next place [...] There is no scale without people at every level and new relationships that take time to develop.

He contrasted this approach with the software development model, which relies on upfront investment and minimal ongoing engagement. Watkins affirmed the efficacy of the model developed through inquiryHub in his district, highlighting the role of Penuel and his team in expertly designing a project that facilitated meaningful community engagement. Watkins emphasized the important benefits of having research that demonstrated the outcomes related to teaching and learning through observations of meaningful shifts in teaching and student experiences. These data helped Watkins communicate with senior leaders in his own district about the importance of continuing the work and contributed to the curriculum's adoption outside of Colorado. This work requires committed community partners who are deeply integrated into the project and who remain engaged over a long term, amidst inevitable turnover, noted Watkins.

BUILDING COMMUNITY CAPACITY FOR AGENCY

Lockett discussed methods that can empower community partners to engage universities and other institutions with agency, highlighting four key components she uses in community training. Lockett, an artist with more than 22 years of experience as an educational practitioner, first noted that she uses art in its most expansive form to connect with people, by using her creativity to translate research into a form that is relatable and accessible to the community.

Second, Lockett noted her efforts to create an inviting atmosphere for community participants, helping them interact with researchers confidently and courageously. "I'm the bridge and the guide across the bridge to academia because I know how to sit in both spaces," she said.

Third, Lockett aims to "translate the language of research." This necessitates cultural sensitivity, she noted, explaining that the language used in research can carry significant weight and may need to be adjusted to respect community members' experiences. For example, she prefers the term "experience" over "project," to avoid the negative connotations associated with the trauma-laden term for housing developments in her community. Finally, Lockett explained that lifting up and honoring community expertise and experiences can erode distrust and help people to feel more comfortable and valued as research practitioners.

DISCUSSION

Challenges in Co-Design and Funding

Rick Tankersley, vice president for research and graduate studies at Portland State University, pointed out a significant challenge faced by researchers: While the co-design process is crucial for building trust and effective community partnerships, it often does not align well with funding processes. The expectation of funders that evidence-based designs be largely established at the time of proposal submission conflicts with co-design as an integral part of project development, he said.

Acknowledging this challenge, Penuel agreed that research-practice partnerships often survive *despite* the existing funding infrastructure rather than because of it. Receiving funding for community-engaged or partnership research, he said, is an art that requires focusing on the evidence base for the proposed approach and presenting a clear plan for achieving the project's goals—although he acknowledged that this approach is not always successful. Penuel suggested that funders could think about community-engaged projects differently; for example, they could determine whether a proposal is justified based on evidence of the community's need and desire for the intervention.

Binns affirmed Penuel's assessment, noting that his desired first step in planning the collaborative proposal with Lockett was to develop relationships within the community. "I really wish we could have had funding to just be on the ground, working together side by side, getting our hands dirty together, and learning from each other. That's what I wish we could have started with. So that was very hard to navigate."

Entry Points for Engaged Research

The discussion shifted to the entry points for engaged research, including co-design—namely, where it starts and how people begin the process. In the early stages of a collaborative project, universities need to be open and available to the community, Lockett said. She explained that her relationship with White at UNC Charlotte allowed her to communicate her community's needs and find support mechanisms in the university. Continued "open door access" as well as university support throughout the project foster collective success, she added.

White noted the frequent mention made during the workshop of individuals with official or unofficial navigator and facilitator roles—people who can serve as crucial entry points for engaged work by connecting researchers with communities. "This is a skill that comes with some experience and expertise," he said, noting that institutions that do not have

VALUING DIVERSE FORMS OF EXPERTISE *57*

dedicated staff for this purpose could benefit from identifying individuals, both in the institution and in the community, who can serve as connectors.

Revolutionizing Scholar Training

Noting the lack of educational opportunities available to teach scholars about engaged research, a participant asked the panel to consider which key capacities, infrastructure, or components need to be developed to better equip researchers to participate in such work.

Lockett suggested the need for vertical alignment in the education system starting from K–12, preparing learners early on for engaged research and community collaboration. "This needs to be a throughline in all of our education systems—formal, informal, private, everywhere," Lockett said. "Our nation could be doing a much better job at this, and we are going to be the ones to step up to that challenge and show them how." One important learning involves valuing qualitative research equally to quantitative research, she added. "I think those stories that live in the community, if we only understood how to take [those] data and really make [them] matter, that's the revolution."

Measuring Success by Community Impact

When asked to identify the key outcomes they seek to elevate in their engaged partnerships, panelists focused on community impact. Such impact stems from deep relationships and the insights provided through the meaningful participation of community partners, including co-design work, noted Binns. Lockett added that impact also necessitates effective implementation of community-driven solutions. Watkins and Penuel concurred, noting that complex outcomes, such as improving epistemic justice in science classrooms, necessitate systems transformation—large-scale changes that can only be achieved through multiple intermediate outcomes.

Evolving Ethical Standards for Community-Engaged Research

Providing a historical perspective on ethical shifts in research practices, a participant noted that the *Belmont Report*[4] marked a significant change in biomedical research, resulting in an emphasis on individual autonomy and consent. He suggested that today's engaged research introduces a new ethical challenge: meaningfully incorporating community consent and participation.

---

[4] Office of the Secretary. (1979). *The Belmont Report: Ethical principles and guidelines for the protection of human subjects of research*. The National Commission for the Protection of Human Subjects of Biomedical and Behavioral Research. https://www.hhs.gov/ohrp/regulations-and-policy/belmont-report/index.html

Penuel noted that emerging models from Indigenous communities, including involvement of community elders and data sovereignty initiatives, focus on ethical considerations of consent and participation in engaged research. He further suggested that ethical issues faced in artificial intelligence and other newly emerging fields, such as questions of data ownership, could provide insights.

White questioned how engaging communities as individuals rather than as collective entities affects the approach to ethical research partnerships. Communities are not monolithic, Lockett responded, voicing her opinion that the value and tone of both individual and collective engagements need to be considered.

Addressing Skepticism

In addressing the skepticism researchers might face when advocating for engaged research, White asked panelists to provide insights on responding to those who question the necessity and feasibility of such work.

Regarding skepticism at the community level, Binns used the lack of trust observed during the rollout of the COVID-19 mRNA vaccine as an example. He noted that community outreach efforts need to extend beyond the superficial to establish or rebuild trust, explaining that this realization encouraged him and his team to embrace discomfort and work toward building trust through genuine engagement: "Now I need to go into these communities and listen. The team I'm working with recognizes that, and a growing number of people recognize that."

Penuel noted continued skepticism around partnership work at the federal level, a sector that, in his opinion, undervalues relationship building in engaged research. Addressing federal skepticism necessitates a broad set of measurable outcomes, Penuel said, including demonstrated solutions to communities' and educational systems' problems, increased trust, changed relationships, and the capacity for joint work. Lockett added another outcome—sourcing and resourcing community efforts. She pointed out that many communities are already working to solve their problems but lack the necessary resources to scale effective solutions.

7

Aligning Core Values and Measurements

Building institutional capacity for engaged research requires moving beyond traditional metrics focused on inputs and outputs—such as funding, students, patents, papers, and publications—to focus on outcomes that truly matter to people and communities. "How do we move from valuing what we measure to measuring what we value?" asked Mahmud Farooque, planning committee member and associate director of the Consortium for Science, Policy and Outcomes. Ideas for addressing this challenge were the focus of a presentation, interactive activities, and discussions.

ENGAGING COMMUNITIES AND CO-DEVELOPING A MEASURE OF TRUST AND TRUSTWORTHINESS

Nadine Barrett, professor of social sciences and health policy and senior associate dean of community engagement and equity in research at Atrium Health Wake Forest School of Medicine, served as a provocateur for this workshop session. She spoke of the early lessons she learned from her mentors, particularly her mother and grandmother, who taught her the value of listening and understanding diverse perspectives and influenced her dedication to community engagement.

Characteristics of Successful Engagement

Barrett highlighted several important characteristics of mature engaged relationships and community partnerships that should underpin both community engagement and meaningful measurement of engaged research:

- *Community expertise*: Community members need to be recognized as experts, stressing that the word "expert" comes from "experience," which communities often possess. Failing to recognize community expertise, she said, misses the opportunity to capitalize on the potential of true partnerships to create meaningful change.
- *Trust*: Although researchers frequently ask how they can build trust in communities, Barrett suggested that the more pertinent question is how researchers and institutions can *become more trustworthy*. Approaching communities with the aim of building trust—instead of focusing on the actions that researchers and institutions need to take to be trustworthy—implies that the community has a problem that needs to be fixed, she explained. Because many systems have historically been untrustworthy, particularly to marginalized and minoritized groups, an inward examination with community insights and expertise is critical to make systemic and organizational change toward trustworthiness.
- *Financial investment*: "We invest in what we value," Barrett said, pointing out that true engagement requires investment at all levels—from federal funding to small foundation grants. "If we really believe and we value community engagement, we're going to invest in it. If your [funding or research] portfolio is not looking like that [by being diverse and reflecting the importance of community engagement], then you already have answered your own question," she noted.
- *Words that matter*: Words have power, Barrett emphasized, criticizing the continued use of terms like "subjects" to describe research participants, which dehumanizes and undermines their contributions. She advocated for referring to community members as colleagues and partners—words that better recognize their collaboration and vital expertise. Barrett intentionally uses such words as community leaders or community colleagues to refer to her partners.
- *Interpersonal elements*: As with personal relationships, noted Barrett, true research partnerships involve honesty, openness, respect, compromise, transparency, and a willingness to ask and listen to difficult questions. If we do not ask hard questions, "we never find out where we need to be, how we need to grow, and in what ways," Barrett said.

Ultimately, an important measure of institutional transformation is the impact that community engagement has on systems, the culture, and the narratives of an organization.

Project ENTRUST

To illustrate building a trustworthy environment in which meaningful partnerships can occur, Barrett shared the process she employed with Project ENTRUST,[1] an ongoing initiative with the aim of addressing trustworthiness and trust in health care and research functions at the Duke University School of Medicine. The project involved

1. engaging more than 40 stakeholders and community experts and over 600 community members in a 12-month process to identify key draft focus areas and questions related to trustworthiness in research and health care at Duke;
2. engaging 15 community-based organizations, with "studios" for community members to provide insights on trust and trustworthiness, with full compensation, as a way for Duke to hear more community perspectives about this important work toward systems transformation in these care areas;
3. convening a 20+ person community stakeholder advisory board; and
4. focusing research on systemic and structural racism and inequities in health.

Describing these steps, she noted that leadership participation and support from multiple departments, as well as from the highest levels of the institution, were crucial for driving the effort forward. Along with community members, Project ENTRUST engaged patients and "invisible" Duke health employees, including environmental services personnel, medical assistants, and food service workers. Overlap can exist between these groups, Barrett pointed out: "We talk about the community as if they are only outside and they do not work inside our organizations, and we have to recognize that [they are inside as well]."

Community partners took the lead at every step of Project ENTRUST, Barrett explained, from defining the study's purpose and goals, to calling for a survey and designing it, to interpreting data. The survey measured

- demographic data,
- source of care,
- barriers to care,
- views on the research enterprise and the institution,
- attitudes toward trustworthiness of institutional research and researchers,
- avoidance of care,
- clinical interactions and health care trustworthiness,

---

[1] See https://ctsi.duke.edu/project-entrust

- experiences of discrimination and bias,
- institutional and organizational trust, and
- trustworthiness of the institution as a community partner.

Over an 8-week period, 6,243 participants representing patients, employees, community residents, and community-based organizations completed the survey. It was particularly powerful to capture the thousands of stories of both trust and mistrust that people shared through the survey, explained Barrett. Moreover, people not only shared their experiences but also offered potential solutions. Then, instead of the traditional approach in which researchers analyze data, draw conclusions, and present results to the community, community partners interpreted the qualitative and quantitative data and provided their insights and recommended solutions in community town halls that included smaller breakout groups.

This approach led to actionable community-driven outcomes addressing such issues as discrimination, bias, and the overall patient and community experiences in health care, research, and partnerships. "[Duke and the community] are actually now working together toward creating the kind of change needed to truly transform the organization from the outside in instead of from the inside out. Centering community insights and expertise is necessary to meaningfully advance trust and trustworthiness in our organizations and create a more equitable, inclusive health care and research environment," Barrett stated.

PARTICIPANTS' IDEAS FOR MEASURES

Farooque invited participants to imagine a world in which metrics are designed to capture what is truly valued, focusing on outcomes and incorporating qualitative measures. Through an interactive activity, participants shared ideas on measures, processes, and outcomes that could be established to align metrics of excellence and success with institutional key values; those ideas are in Appendix C. Emily Ozer, planning committee member and clinical and community psychologist and professor of public health at the University of California, Berkeley, highlighted the wealth of existing measurement tools mentioned in participants' comments. She emphasized the need for a meta-network to share these resources across disciplines. Focusing on adapting and co-designing existing measures to fit researchers' specific contexts could avoid the need to reinvent methods, she said.

Several key points related to measuring trustworthiness and relationship building were raised by the participants:

- Eboné Lockett, chief executive officer and principal consultant of Harvesting Humanity, emphasized the importance of community-led professional development as a means of building trustworthiness

ALIGNING CORE VALUES AND MEASUREMENTS

and relationships while bolstering the expertise of both academics and community partners.

- Prajakta Adsul, assistant professor in the Department of Internal Medicine at the University of New Mexico, called attention to the Engage for Equity project (see Chapter 4), which adapted principles of trustworthiness from the Association of American Medical Colleges to create a scale for measuring trustworthiness in communication between researchers and community partners.
- Marisol Morales, executive director of the Carnegie Elective Classifications and assistant vice president at the American Council on Education, noted that universities often have "boundary spanners"—people with established relationships with trusted community figures. To enhance trust and engagement, researchers need to engage boundary spanners to bridge gaps between academic and community settings, she said. Leveraging students' dual identities as community members and scholars can also build trust between institutions and communities, she pointed out.

A participant mentioned that the success of collaborative relationships can also be gauged by the level of voluntary participation and interest—increasing demand for collaborative opportunities is a strong indicator of success and engagement, he noted.

Farooque concluded the session by reflecting on the dual purpose of measurement. While measurement can be used to prove success, it is also of critical use in facilitating learning, ensuring that engaged research practices are "moving at the pace of trust."

8

Next Steps for Action

To provide a framework for participants' visions of the future of engaged scholarship and to help identify systems needed for institutional change, Tim Eatman, planning committee member and dean of the Honors Living-Learning Community and professor of urban education at Rutgers University–Newark, presented a conceptual map illustrating the key elements of publicly engaged scholarship, a term that includes engaged research.

Specifically, publicly engaged scholarship

- urges a "continuum of scholarship" paradigm, ranging from traditional to publicly engaged, which recognizes and respects all kinds of work and implies interdisciplinarity;
- requires "prophetic imagining," or visionary foresight;
- hinges on clear and adaptable definitions, which lead to equitable and well-articulated evaluation criteria;
- manifests in trusting relationships and public-good impact;
- depends on democratic practice and full participation;
- embraces creative cultural organizing;
- rejects the exclusivity and sufficiency of the "ivory tower" mindset; and
- may lead to nontraditional career paths and scholarly products.

66 BUILDING INSTITUTIONAL CAPACITY FOR ENGAGED RESEARCH

Participants were then given time for individual reflection on two guiding questions before discussing their ideas:

1. What will engaged research look like when organizations are shifted, infrastructure is built, and networks have been coordinated?
2. What actions could be taken right now to achieve that vision?

DISCUSSION

Participants shared ideas about key elements that would be in place in a hypothetical future in which capacity for engaged research is established, valued, supported, and normalized at scale. To guide the discussion, Eatman encouraged participants to harness their capacity for "prophetic imagination." "I think that's really our challenge," he said. "I think it's a failure of imagination." Likening prophetic imagination to the boundless curiosity of a child taking their first steps, he said, "If I want a different future, I've got to think about taking breaking points and making them making points. Turning breaking points into making points [is] the work of imagining." Visions included a future in which civic engagement is consistently valued and modeled in education, funding systems support engaged scholarship, and institutional structures fully incorporate epistemic justice.

Modeling Civic Engagement in Education

A participant remarked that, in his vision of the future, engaged educators will knowingly serve as models for their students, empowering the next generation of researchers to carry engagement practices into various sectors—thereby changing organizational cultures. In addition to teaching students how to be responsible communicators, which can build trust and understanding with communities, educator modeling can also teach students to question how research priorities are decided, he said.

A participant who works with seniors in science, technology, engineering, and mathematics (STEM) education concurred, noting that the main modeling he has observed illustrates only the traditional path of working in a lab and going on to earn a Ph.D.—most students are unaware of community engagement opportunities because they do not see them modeled, he said. Furthermore, he noted the imbalance in credit allocation between STEM courses, which are generally 3–4 credits, and courses focusing on community engagement or science communication, which might only consist of a 1-credit requirement over 4 years. This imbalance sends a message about the value of community engagement in the academic curriculum, he stated, highlighting his vision of curriculum reform to better integrate STEM with community engagement.

Another participant expanded on the theme of increased integration of civic engagement and engaged research in undergraduate education. She shared her experience at a college where long-term commitments to community co-created projects were institutionalized across multiple courses and disciplines—an approach that educates future citizens and researchers to collaborate effectively in communities. Eatman followed up by pointing to the Reggio Emilia Approach[1] as an example of instilling collaborative values in children through the education process.

Redesigned Funding Models

Noting the current need to "almost retrofit our funding processes so that they support community-led organizations," a participant from a funding organization shared that her vision of the future involves new funding processes specifically designed to support community-led research. To further this vision, the competition component of funding could be eliminated by directly allocating funds to communities and allowing them to innovate, she suggested.

Another participant suggested that linking scholarly outputs to U.N. Sustainable Development Goals (SDGs)[2] could help scientists—including many workshop participants—align their academic work with broader global priorities. When included in funding proposals, such links to the larger global context of SDGs can enhance researchers' chances of receiving funding, he said.

Redesigned Institutional Structures and Epistemic Justice

Several participants proposed visions of the future that involved redesigning institutional structures.

- One participant proposed a vision in which academic institutions fully integrate interdisciplinarity, which would include community involvement. She noted that while interdisciplinarity is often discussed, it is rarely fully implemented in practice.
- Another participant suggested that institutions could redesign current guidelines, such as diversity, equity, and inclusion policies, to integrate engaged research. Incorporation into institution-wide policies could lead to a future in which entire universities, rather than isolated departments or scholars, prioritize community engagement in their work.

---

[1] See https://www.reggiochildren.it/en/reggio-emilia-approach/

[2] See https://unfoundation.org/what-we-do/issues/sustainable-development-goals/u-s-leadership-on-the-sdgs/?gad_source=1&gclid=CjwKCAjw2Je1BhAgEiwAp3KY76jmuXxCPNxGWteGczOPvkL—3RQDX0NmrgigCr3V7_5tFvTFFs2IRoCHv8QAvD_BwE

- Michael Rios, vice provost of public scholarship and professor of human ecology at the University of California, Davis, said his vision of the future called for reimagining the knowledge enterprise, shifting the system from epistemic harm to inclusion and justice: "We are tinkering around a framework that's developed over time. And in a sense, that has to fundamentally change." Achieving this vision would require shifting away from the traditional framework of research, teaching, and service to a more holistic approach that values all types of impacts equally, he said.
- Lina Dostilio, vice chancellor of engagement and community affairs and associate professor in the School of Education at the University of Pittsburgh, brought a chancellor's perspective to Rios's proposed framework, envisioning two structural features that would make future engaged research dramatically different than it is today: (a) providing community-based knowledge producers with "full identity status privilege in knowledge production," transcending their current appointments as fellows or visiting researchers; and (b) creating a flexible system that can be highly responsive to urgent local issues, similar to the quick pivot in priorities seen during the COVID-19 pandemic.

NEXT STEPS FOR INCREASING COORDINATION AND CAPACITY BUILDING

Participants chose to participate in one of the four breakout groups that reflected the main topics of interest: building the scholarship of engaged research and equipping individuals and partners; organizational and culture change; artifacts, metrics, and incentives; and funding for research and sustainability. Each group was asked to consider the following prompts:

- What immediate actions would you prioritize? (Round robin)
- What actions if adopted do you think would be the most impactful?
- What actors should take that action?
- What can you do in your role about this?
- What would you prioritize for coordination, and who should be a part of that?

Planning committee members facilitated these discussions and reported the ideas from their breakout groups to the full workshop, which are summarized below. More detailed artifacts from these discussions are available on the project website.

Building Scholarship and
Equipping Individuals and Partners

Elsa Falkenburger, director of the Community Engagement Resource Center at the Urban Institute, reported on ideas to prepare community partners and researchers for engaged work and to facilitate collaboration and inclusivity in partnerships. Several actionable steps were identified:

- Assume the topic at hand is already being discussed at the community level and invest in existing conversations and efforts.
- Focus on community action instead of representation—ensure work is led from the community.
- Take active responsibility for policy implementation steps included in reports.
- Recognize and integrate experiences of colleagues and community members, blurring the line between community and professional expertise.
- Ensure fair compensation for community members at all phases of work, similar to that received by professional sources of expertise.
- Develop courses based on existing community expertise and history, allowing community members to teach and ground students in local context.
- Value and incorporate students' skills, identities, and experiences as strengths in collaborative, participatory research with the community.

Organizational and Culture Change

Emily Ozer, planning committee member and clinical and community psychologist and professor of public health at the University of California, Berkeley, and Mahmud Farooque, associate director of the consortium for science, policy and outcomes at Arizona State University, reported on the key action steps to address issues of organizational and institutional culture change that arose from their breakout groups.

- Encourage co-learning in diverse meta-networks of participants, including university presidents, funders, faculty, and community members, and explore ways to sustain this collaborative space.
- Learn from existing metrics, measures, and organizational structures to streamline efforts instead of "reinventing the wheel."
- Prioritize clear, consistent language and concise mission statements, modeled after Promotion & Tenure – Innovation &

70 BUILDING INSTITUTIONAL CAPACITY FOR ENGAGED RESEARCH

Entrepreneurship (see Chapter 5) or similar initiatives, to enhance communication.

- Propose a standing committee on science communication at the National Academies of Sciences, Engineering, and Medicine and seek funding for a consensus study on community-engaged research. Such a committee could
  - establish scholarly standards for community-engaged research, recognizing the need for diverse perspectives and avoiding a one-size-fits-all approach;
  - engage opt-in participants from the current workshop to form a steering committee for the new committee;
  - develop shared principles, goals, agreements, objectives, and timelines for the coalition;
  - leverage existing connections to invite others to join the coalition;
  - provide support and advocacy outside the coalition by offering consultation, advice, and referrals;
  - act as ambassadors and advocates;
  - ensure equitable access for the next generation; and
  - communicate valuation of all forms of knowledge and learning.

Artifacts, Metrics, and Incentives

Elyse Aurbach, director for public engagement and research impacts at the University of Michigan, described priorities and action steps related to artifacts, metrics, and incentives from that breakout group.

- Push for funding specifically dedicated to assessment, especially during post-award periods when impact may take time to manifest.
- Equip and compensate community partners as co-equal designers of the assessment process.
- Identify and utilize promising assessment models from various disciplines.
- Facilitate field-wide sense-making and create on-ramps that familiarize newcomers with established assessment practices.
- Develop a menu of core metrics or common data elements to support assessment across institutional and funding levels.
- Address challenges related to updating, sustaining, and determining the best host for supporting ongoing assessment work.

Funding for Research and Sustainability

Susan Renoe, associate vice chancellor at University of Missouri, reported on the next steps related to addressing challenges related to funding for sustainability that emerged from that breakout group.

- Create supportive professional development environments within institutions to enable training for principal investigators on such topics as sustainability, coalition building, community partnership building, leadership skills, and fundraising.
- Involve community experts in the development and evaluation of requests for proposals, to ensure diverse perspectives and innovative approaches.
- Share data and metrics with funders to support investment in research initiatives.
- Embed support mechanisms within funding structures or encourage researchers to include such supports in their teams.

Appendix A

Workshop Agenda

THURSDAY, JUNE 13, 2024

8:30 a.m.   **Light Breakfast**

9:00 a.m.   **Welcome Remarks and Goals for the Workshop**

Heidi Schweingruber, Board on Science Education, National Academies of Sciences, Engineering, and Medicine; Susan D. Renoe, University of Missouri, Planning Committee Chair

9:20 a.m.   **Exploring Participant Roles and Goals**

Meeting participants will engage in an interactive activity to explore

- the complexity of the research ecosystem and affirm the multiple roles required to make it work;
- participant roles, interests, and motivations for participation; and
- opportunities to make connections across and within roles and sectors.

9:30 a.m.   **Why Is Engaged Research Important?**

Moderator: Kimberly Jones, Howard University, Planning Committee Member

A panel of three teams of researchers and their community partners will illustrate what can be achieved through engaged research in ways that benefit communities, researchers, and society. Presentations and moderated

74   BUILDING INSTITUTIONAL CAPACITY FOR ENGAGED RESEARCH

discussion will explore key tensions they encountered, and approaches they used to overcome those challenges.

Teams:

Project: PAR4 FED Success

Jennifer Wilding, Kansas City Federal Reserve Bank, and *John James, Wendell Phillips Neighborhood Association*

Project: Healthy Environments Partnership

Amy Schulz, University of Michigan, and *Angela Reyes, Detroit Hispanic Development Corporation*

Project: Northeastern University / City of Boston's Department of Youth Engagement and Employment to Reduce Inequality

Alicia Modestino, Northeastern University, and *Rashad Cope, City of Boston*

10:20 a.m.	Panel and Audience Discussion

10:35 a.m.	Break

10:50 a.m.	Identifying Promising Pathways Forward: Addressing Key Tensions in the System

Speakers: Elyse Aurbach, University of Michigan, and *Emily Ozer, University of California, Berkeley, Planning Committee Members*

Insights across two major landscape reviews offer insights into what has been learned about existing challenges and solutions, and how these are shaped by broader forces and parts of the larger ecosystem.

Presenters will also describe how these reviews have shaped the framing for the workshop around identifying successful approaches for addressing key tensions that have limited progress in building capacity for engaged research.

11:10 a.m.	Participants' Discussion

11:25 a.m.	Addressing Tensions Related to Values, Traditions, and Priorities

Moderator: Mahmud Farooque, Arizona State University, Planning Committee Member

APPENDIX A   75

Engaged research can often be at odds with the traditional ways that research institutions are structured and what is valued inside and outside of these institutions. In a set of brief presentations designed to spark participant engagement, three panelists will describe innovative approaches they have implemented to address these types of tensions.

Panelists: Tabia Akintobi, Morehouse School of Medicine; Michael Rios, University of California, Davis; Mary Jo Callan, Brown University

11:55 a.m.   **Panel and Participant Discussion**

12:15 p.m.   **Lunch**

1:15 p.m.   **Addressing Tensions Related to Infrastructure**

Moderator: Elsa Falkenburger, Urban Institute, Planning Committee Member

In a set of brief presentations designed to spark participant engagement, three panelists will describe their innovative approaches to engaged research that involved new operational processes, procedures, or organizational structures. They will describe approaches for working within legal and accounting guardrails while streamlining the "pain points" that currently undermine partnered research.

Panelists: Prajakta Adsul, University of New Mexico School of Medicine; Lina Dostilio, University of Pittsburgh; Adam Parris, ICF

1:45 p.m.   **Panel and Participant Discussion**

2:05 p.m.   **Interactive Activity: Focus on Generating Solutions**

Participants will expand on the ideas discussed around the tensions discussed and surface further innovations/bright spots that could be adopted or require coordinated solutions.

2:50 p.m.   **Identifying Common Themes and Gaps**

Moderator: Elyse Aurbach, University of Michigan, Planning Committee Member

In a plenary discussion, participants will offer their reflections on emerging themes and identify any gaps that may need further discussion.

76   *BUILDING INSTITUTIONAL CAPACITY FOR ENGAGED RESEARCH*

3:20 p.m.   Break

3:30 p.m.   **Aligning Mission and Incentives: Valuing and Prioritizing Engaged Research**

Moderator: Susan D. Renoe, University of Missouri, Planning Committee Chair

Building on earlier sessions, a panel of five leaders from different sectors will participate in a moderated panel discussion focused on aligning incentives for successful engaged research. Panelists will discuss topics, such as

- the role of engaged research as part of being an excellent institution,
- demand for engaged research,
- promotion and tenure,
- incentivizing engaged research at scale, and
- measuring engaged research.

Panelists: *Cheryl Boyce, National Institutes of Health; Rich Carter, PTIE and Oregon State University; KerryAnn O'Meara, Teachers College, Columbia University; Marisol Morales, American Council on Education; Toby Smith, Association of American Universities*

4:25 p.m.   Audience Discussion

4:45 p.m.   Reflections on the Day

Neeli Bendapudi, President, Penn State University

5:00 p.m.   Look-Ahead to Day 2

Timothy Eatman, Rutgers University–Newark, Planning Committee Member

5:10 p.m.   Networking

Participants will have the opportunity to enjoy light refreshments and talk informally with other attendees and speakers.

6:00 p.m.   Adjourn

APPENDIX A 77

FRIDAY, JUNE 14, 2024

8:30 a.m.   **Light Breakfast**

9:00 a.m.   **Welcome Remarks**

Erwin Gianchandani, TIP Directorate, National Science Foundation

9:15 a.m.   **Valuing Diverse Forms of Expertise**

Moderator: Byron White, University of North Carolina–Charlotte, Planning Committee Member

What would it look like to center community interests and aims, share power, and co-create knowledge to achieve meaningful societal impact? Acknowledging that too often science extracts, excludes, and falls short of its promises, panelists will share their experiences in building true partnerships, and bringing together diverse forms of knowledge, reflecting on what supports are needed to allow this to occur at scale.

Panelists: Ian Binns, UNC Charlotte; Eboné Lockett, Harvesting Humanity; William Penuel, University of Colorado Boulder; Douglas Watkins, Denver Public Schools

10:05 a.m.   **Participant Discussion**

10:20 a.m.   **Break**

10:30 a.m.   **Aligning Core Values and Measurement**

Moderator: Mahmud Farooque, Arizona State University, Planning Committee Member

Provocateur: Nadine Barrett, Wake Forest University

This session will ask participants to consider how core values can align with metrics and measures of excellence and success for researchers, communities and other partners, and institutions.

11:15 a.m.   **A Vision for the Future**

Tim Eatman, Rutgers University–Newark, Planning Committee Member

Engaged research has many different aims. It offers opportunities for communities to work together with researchers to improve outcomes, for researchers and practitioners to co-create new approaches, for developing needed policy solutions, and for accelerating the innovation process. Participants will reflect on a vision of the future in which the needed capacity for engaged research has been built and is valued, supported, and normalized at scale.

12:00 p.m.   Lunch

1:00 p.m.   **Putting It All Together: Generating Next Steps for Increasing Coordination and Capacity Building**

In small groups, participants will prioritize and generate ideas for increasing coordination and capacity building for engaged research, focusing on the roles of different actors in the ecosystem.

2:15 p.m.   **Summary and Final Reflections**

Planning committee members report on the prioritized actions and opportunities for coordination generated by the small groups and offer a final wrap-up.

3:00 p.m.   **Adjourn**

Appendix B

Biosketches of Planning Committee Members and Speakers

PLANNING COMMITTEE

SUSAN D. RENOE (*Chair*, she/her/hers) is associate vice chancellor at the University of Missouri (MU). She also serves as executive director of the National Science Foundation-funded Center for Advancing Research Impact in Society and is an assistant professor of strategic communication in the MU School of Journalism. She was elected an AAAS Fellow in 2021 and a member of the Academy of Community Engagement Scholarship in 2024. Renoe serves on several advisory boards including the Committee on Equal Opportunities in Science and Engineering, the Network for Advancing & Evaluating the Societal Impact of Science, and the Research Impact Assessment Advisory Board for the Centres de Recerca de Catalunya. She received both B.A. and M.A. degrees in anthropology from MU, and both M.A. and Ph.D. degrees in education from the University of California, Santa Barbara.

ELYSE L. AURBACH (she/her/hers) is a public engagement professional and researcher. As director for public engagement and research impacts in the University of Michigan's Office of Research, she leads strategy and a team to support university faculty in their public engagement efforts. Aurbach creates communities, programs, and products that maximize assets and address needs to support scholars in engaging with different publics. She specializes in translating research into useful tools for practice, building effective training and capacity-building programs, and developing frameworks that synthesize scholarship and practitioner knowledge to help university and public engagement systems evolve. Aurbach served as a civic science fellow with the Association of Public and Land-grant Universities, where she led the Modernizing Scholarship for the Public Good initiative, offering guidance to public research universities on ways that they can support scholars and advance public impact research and other forms of public engagement, and diversity, equity, and inclusion. She also led a number of projects to improve science communication and public engagement, including developing and teaching communication courses in person and online, co-bossing with Nerd Nite Ann Arbor, and co-founding and directing RELATE, a science communication and public engagement organization. Aurbach was a National Science Foundation graduate research fellow, a finalist for the AAAS Early Career Award for Public Engagement with Science, and an Advancing Research Impact in Society fellow. She holds a Ph.D. in neuroscience.

TIMOTHY K. EATMAN (he/him/his) is an educational sociologist and publicly engaged scholar, serving as the inaugural dean of the Honors Living-Learning Community and professor of urban education at Rutgers University–Newark. Prior to this current appointment, his primary network of scholarly operation and leadership was with the national consortium Imagining America: Artists and Scholars in Public Life, serving first as director of research and ultimately as faculty co-director. Now in his second term on the board of directors of the American Association of Colleges and Universities (AAC&U), Eatman serves as chair of the membership committee and as board chair. Also with AAC&U, he serves as a faculty member of the Institute on High-Impact Practices and Student Success. Eatman is a member of the National Advisory Committee for the Carnegie Elective Classification for Community Engagement and the National Advisory Board for Bringing Theory to Practice. In addition, he currently serves as national co-chair of the Urban Research-Based Action Network. Most recently, Eatman has served as a member of the Institutional Change Grant review panel for the William T. Grant Foundation. He has written several book chapters and research reports including the widely cited *Scholarship in Public: Knowledge Creation and Tenure Policy in the Engaged University*, a seminal report on faculty rewards and publicly engaged scholarship. Eatman earned his B.A. (Pace University), an M.Ed. (Howard University) in the field of education, and a Ph.D. in educational policy from the University of Illinois-Urbana Champaign.

ELSA FALKENBURGER (she/her/hers) is a senior fellow and director of the Community Engagement Resource Center at the Urban Institute Center in the Division on Race and Equity. She also co-directs the Contextual Analysis and Methods of Participatory Engagement project at

APPENDIX B   81

the U.S. Department of Health and Human Services Office of Planning, Research and Evaluation, and a participatory evaluation for the Partnership for Equitable and Resilient Communities, an initiative of the Melville Charitable Trust. Formerly, Falkenburger was co–principal investigator of the Promoting Adolescent Sexual Health and Safety project, a 12-year sustained partnership with the DC Housing Authority and community-based organizations and residents to design and evaluate programming for teens. She regularly provides technical assistance and trainings, develops practical guides to implementing community-engaged methods focused on equity, and consults on the institutionalization of participatory methods. Falkenburger has a B.A. in economics from Boston College and an M.P.A. from the University of Texas at Austin.

MAHMUD FAROOQUE (he/him/his) is the associate director of the Consortium for Science, Policy and Outcomes; a clinical professor in the School for the Future of Innovation in Society; and a senior global futures scholar in the Julie Ann Wrigley Global Futures Laboratory at the Arizona State University. Previously, he was the deputy director of policy programs at the New York Academy of Science, director of collaborative research at City University of New York, associate director for research development at Northwestern University, and managing director of the U.S. Department of Transportation's Region V University Research Center at Purdue University. Farooque's expertise focuses on innovation systems, research management, knowledge co-production, policy entrepreneurship, and participatory technology assessment. He is the principal coordinator of Expert and Citizen Assessment of Science and Technology (ECAST)— a distributed network of universities, science centers, and policy research organizations for engaging the public in science and technology policy and decision making. ECAST has organized more than 50 informed and inclusive public deliberations across the country on issues from biodiversity and planetary defense to community resilience, climate intervention, and gene editing. Farooque is an editorial board member on the *Journal for Technology Assessment in Theory and Practice* and advisory board member of the Institute for a Sustainable Earth at George Mason University. He has an M.P.A. in technology and information policy and a Ph.D. in public policy.

KIMBERLY L. JONES (she/her/hers) currently serves as associate dean for research and graduate education (College of Engineering and Architecture) as well as professor and chair (Department of Civil and Environmental Engineering) at Howard University. Jones's areas of research expertise are in environmental justice, water quality and reuse, resource recovery, environmental management, and environmental nanotechnology. She has served on the Chartered Science Advisory Board of the U.S. Environmental Protection Agency, where she chaired the Drinking Water Committee and was liaison to the National Drinking Water Advisory Council. Jones is an alternate commissioner of the Interstate Commission on the Potomac River Basin in Washington, DC, where she chairs the committee on justice, equity, diversity, and inclusion. She also serves on the Center Steering Committee of the Center for the Environmental Implications of Nanotechnology and on the Management Board of the Consortium for Risk Evaluation with Stakeholder Participation. Jones has received the Researcher of the Year award from Howard University, a Top Women in Science Award from the National Technical Association, the Outstanding Young Civil Engineer award from University of Illinois Department of Civil and Environmental Engineering, a National Science Foundation CAREER Award, an Outstanding Leadership and Service and Outstanding Faculty Mentor award from Howard University, and Top Women Achievers award from *Essence* magazine. She holds a B.S. in civil engineering from Howard University, an M.S. in civil and environmental engineering from the University of Illinois, and a Ph.D. in environmental engineering from the Johns Hopkins University.

EMILY J. OZER (she/her/hers) is a clinical and community psychologist and professor at the University of California, Berkeley School of Public Health, whose multi-method research focuses on the role of school climate in adolescent development and mental health; psychological resilience; school-based interventions; and youth participatory action research, an equity-focused approach in which youth generate systematic research evidence to address problems they want to improve in their schools and communities. She has been the recipient of multiple national awards for her research, including selection as a fellow of the American Psychological Association, as well as a national mentorship award from the Society for Research on Adolescence. Funded by a William T. Grant Institutional Challenge Grant (co-funded by Doris Duke Foundation), Ozer is actively leading an initiative to strengthen policies and culture to support community-engaged research at Berkeley and on a research-practice partnership with the San Francisco Unified School district to promote student well-being and integrate student-led research in school improvement and equity initiatives. She led a national scan recently released by The Pew Charitable Trusts, sponsored by the Transforming Evidence Funders Network, on innovations in the evaluation of community-engaged and public impact research and has engaged in a range of national and international discussions on the topic. She currently serves as the faculty liaison to the Berkeley Provost on Public Scholarship and Community Engagement. Ozer holds a Ph.D. in psychology from the University of California, Berkeley.

APPENDIX B 83

BYRON P. WHITE (he/him/his) is associate provost for urban research and community engagement at the University of North Carolina (UNC) at Charlotte. He oversees urbanCORE (Community-Oriented Research and Engagement), an office that mobilizes, assesses, and advances efforts that connect the university's research resources to community assets. Prior to joining UNC Charlotte, White was executive director of Strive Partnership, a Cincinnati-based collective impact organization focused on education improvement for urban learners from cradle to career. He previously was vice president for university engagement and chief diversity officer at Cleveland State University, vice chancellor for economic advancement for the University System of Ohio, and associate vice president for community engagement at Xavier University in Cincinnati. White began his career as a newspaper journalist and was as an editorial writer for the *Chicago Tribune* and editor of the *Tribune's* Urban Affairs Team. He has been active in grassroots community development efforts, working with community-based organizations in Cincinnati and on Chicago's West Side through the Asset-Based Community Development Institute. White has a B.A in journalism from Ohio University, an M.A. in social science from the University of Chicago, and a Ph.D. in higher education management from the University of Pennsylvania.

SPEAKERS

PRAJAKTA ADSUL (she/her/hers) is an assistant professor in the Department of Internal Medicine and a member of the Cancer Control and Population Sciences Research Program at the Comprehensive Cancer Center at University of New Mexico (UNM). Most recently, she was nominated to serve as the inaugural director of the newly established Center for Advancing Dissemination and Implementation Science at UNM. Adsul is a primary care physician by training and was a Cancer Prevention Fellow with the Implementation Science team at the National Cancer Institute. As an implementation scientist, she uses community-based and participatory research approaches focused on health equity, often utilizing mixed methods that can help develop and test interventions and implementation strategies in pragmatic studies for cancer prevention and control. Adsul holds an M.P.H. in epidemiology with a focus on behavioral sciences and health education and a Ph.D. in public health.

TABIA H. AKINTOBI (she/her/hers) is professor and chair of the Department of Community Health and Preventive Medicine at Morehouse School of Medicine. She is a globally sought social behavioral scientist and public health practitioner leading or collaborating in community-driven translational research and programs contributing to the eradication of health disparities, thereby advancing community and population health transformation. Akintobi is principal investigator of a Prevention Research Center funded by the Centers for Disease Control and Prevention, designed to advance the art and implementation science of community-based participatory research grounded in community governance. She is also principal investigator, lead, or advisor for other local and national centers, institutes, and networks funded by the National Institute of Diabetes and Digestive and Kidney Diseases, the National Institute on Minority Health and Health Disparities, the National Center for Advancing Translational Sciences, and the U.S. Department of Health and Human Services, among many others. Akintobi received her M.P.H. and Ph.D. from the University of South Florida.

NADINE J. BARRETT (she/her/hers) is a professor in the Department of Social Sciences and Health Policy in the Division of Public Health Sciences, and the inaugural senior associate dean of community engagement and equity in research at Atrium Health Wake Forest School of Medicine, the third largest learning health system in the United States. She is associate director of community outreach and engagement for Wake Forest Comprehensive Cancer Center, and associate director of community engagement in the Clinical and Translational Science Institute and the Maya Angelou Center for Health Equity. Prior to joining Wake Forest, Barrett served in several senior leadership roles at Duke University including as the co-director for equity and stakeholder strategy for Duke Clinical and Translational Science Institute, and the founding director of both the Duke Center for Equity in Research and the nationally awarded Duke Cancer Institute's Office of Health Equity. She completed an M.A. in sociology and social inequities at the University of Central Florida, a joint M.S. in community health sciences and Ph.D. in medical sociology and race and ethnic relations from Texas Woman's University, alongside a National Institutes of Health joint postdoctoral fellowship at the University of North Carolina at Chapel Hill and Duke University.

NEELI BENDAPUDI (she/her/hers) serves as the president of the Pennsylvania State University and leads the university with a vision grounded in the principles of purpose, agility, and opportunity. With a nearly 30-year career in higher education and business, she is recognized as a leading educator, academic, and executive. Bendapudi previously served as president of the University of Louisville, in various leadership positions with the University of Kansas and Ohio State University, and as the executive vice president and chief customer officer for Huntington National Bank. She holds a Ph.D. in marketing and is a noted scholar on the study of consumer behavior in service contexts.

APPENDIX B 85

IAN C. BINNS (he/him/his) is an associate professor of elementary science education in the Department of Reading and Elementary Education at the Cato College of Education at the University of North Carolina at Charlotte. He is also a member of Computational Intelligence to Predict Health and Environmental Risks (CIPHER). As a member of CIPHER, Binns focuses on ways to build and support relationships with various community partners as well as promoting the work done by CIPHER researchers. His research also focuses on the interaction between science and religion with the goal of helping people understand their unique contributions to benefit society. Binns is a co-host of the podcast *Down the Wormhole*, a show exploring the "strange and fascinating relationship between science and religion," and the host of the podcast *de-CIPHERing Infectious Disease*. He holds a Ph.D. in science education from the University of Virginia.

CHERYL ANNE BOYCE (she/her/hers) is the assistant director for re-engineering the research enterprise, National Institutes of Health. She joined the Office of Strategic Coordination to lead the Transformative Research to Address Health Disparities and Advance Health Equity and Community Partnerships to Advance Science for Society programs. Previously, Boyce was the chief of the Implementation Science Branch within the Center for Translation Research and Implementation Science at the National Heart, Lung, and Blood Institute. She completed doctoral studies in clinical psychology at the University of North Carolina at Chapel Hill.

MARY JO CALLAN (she/her/hers) currently serves as the vice president of community engagement for Brown University and executive director of the Swearer Center for Public Service. In this dual role, she leads efforts to integrate fair and sustainable community-engaged teaching, research, learning, and practice in order to advance socially just change. Serving as a member of the President's Cabinet, Callan provides strategic leadership to grow positive place-based engagement within Providence and Rhode Island by coordinating, developing, and stewarding partnerships, programs, and investments. Prior to her role at Brown University, she served as the director of the Edward Ginsberg Center, a community engagement center at the University of Michigan, and in leadership roles within K–12 schools, local government, and the nonprofit sector. Callan's scholarly work and practice has focused on partnerships between universities and social and public sector organizations, with a particular emphasis on equity and reciprocity in these partnerships. Callan earned bachelor's and master's degrees at the University of Michigan, and a doctorate in educational policy and leadership at the College of William and Mary.

RICH G. CARTER (he/him/his) is professor of chemistry and faculty lead for innovation excellence at Oregon State University. He leads the National Science Foundation-supported national Promotion & Tenure – Innovation & Entrepreneurship organization that has developed consensus recommendations through its 65+ university coalition on how to inclusively recognize innovation and entrepreneurship (I&E) impact by university faculty. In recent years, this work has included working closely with institutions to support culture change around I&E on their campuses. In addition, Carter is co-founder and chief executive officer of Valliscor—an organofluorine-focused chemical manufacturing company that supplies the pharmaceutical and semiconductor sectors. He holds a Ph.D. in chemistry.

RASHAD O. COPE (he/him/his) is deputy chief of the Worker Empowerment Cabinet for the City of Boston, where he enhances residents' lives through workforce development, youth employment, and strategic partnerships. He crafts comprehensive strategies to address inequities and improve outcomes for employment and career awareness programs, while supporting workforce training, learning and job readiness, financial services, and workforce grant initiatives. Cope holds an M.B.A. from Fitchburg State University and an M.S. Ed. and Nonprofit Organizational Leadership Graduate Certificate from Boston University Wheelock College of Education and Human Development.

LINA DOSTILIO (she/her/hers) sets and advances the University of Pittsburgh's community engagement agenda and catalyzes community-facing efforts across the university, including place-based engagement efforts, engaged scholarship, strategic partnership development, and community affairs. She is also an associate professor of practice within the Department of Educational Foundations, Organizations, and Policy in the School of Education. Dostilio's research explores the community engagement professional in higher education and hyperlocal, place-based engagement. She serves on the council of experts for the National Science Foundation-funded Center for Advancing Research Impact in Society and the executive committee of the Commission on Economic and Community Engagement at the Association of Public and Land-grant Universities. Dostilio is an inducted member of the Academy of Community Engagement Scholarship, a selective honor recognizing outstanding scholarly contributions to community engagement. She holds a B.A. from the Pennsylvania State University, with both M.A. and Ph.D. degrees from Duquesne University.

ERWIN GIANCHANDANI (he/him/his) is the U.S. National Science Foundation (NSF) assistant director for Technology, Innovation and Partnerships (TIP), leading the newly established TIP directorate. Prior to becoming the assistant director for TIP, he served as the senior advisor for translation,

APPENDIX B   87

innovation and partnerships, where he helped develop plans for the new TIP directorate in collaboration with colleagues at NSF, other government agencies, industry, and academia. Gianchandani was previously the NSF deputy assistant director for Computer and Information Science and Engineering, twice serving as acting assistant director. Before joining NSF in 2012, he was the inaugural director of the Computing Community Consortium, providing leadership to the computing research community in identifying and pursuing bold, high-impact research directions such as health information technology and sustainable computing. Gianchandani received the Distinguished Presidential Rank Award, awarded to members of the federal government's Senior Executive Service for sustained extraordinary accomplishment. He holds a Ph.D. in biomedical engineering from the University of Virginia.

JOHN P. JAMES (he/him/his) is president of the Wendell Phillips Neighborhood Association. He is often dubbed a "collaborator" or "servant leader"— connecting, encouraging, mentoring, and leading others to pursue greater opportunities. James has extensive experience in the information technology field in the private and public sectors, including technology work for the United States Air Force, from which he is retired. He is currently employed by the City of Kansas City, Missouri, as an information technology specialist in its Information Technology Division. James is also an overseer for the Free Churches, working behind the scenes to ensure the smooth operation and management of the organization. He serves as a bishop and the first administrative assistant to the prelate bishop at Victory Way Most High God Free Church.

EBONÉ LOCKETT (she/her/hers) serves as the chief executive officer and principal consultant of Harvesting Humanity, LLC. Harvesting Humanity is a full-service educational and social enterprise engaging, preparing, and positioning local, national, and global "Solutionaries" via a holistically integrated Science, Technology, Reading and Writing, Engineering, Arts, Architecture, Agriculture and Mathematics© experiential, service-learning model. She previously taught secondary English language arts, humanities, and life skills. Lockett is a three-time-consecutive recipient of the Charlotte Hornets Teacher Innovation Grant, winner of an Arts and Science Council Cato Excellence in Teaching Award, and Qatar teacher travel grant recipient. She earned an M.S. degree in educational leadership from Central Connecticut State University with a focus on curriculum and instruction.

ALICIA MODESTINO (she/her/hers) is an associate professor with appointments in the School of Public Policy and Urban Affairs and the

Department of Economics at Northeastern University, where she also serves as the research director of the Dukakis Center for Urban and Regional Policy. Her research focuses on labor market dynamics including skills mismatch, youth labor market attachment, and career pathways. Modestino currently leads a multiyear Institutional Challenge Grant funded by the William T. Grant Foundation to evaluate the Boston Summer Youth Employment Program. Last year, she launched a new initiative across Northeastern's global campus network—Community-to-Community (C2C): Policy Equity for All. Working in partnership with city departments, state agencies, and community-based organizations C2C provides rigorous data and analysis to find solutions to the most urgent public problems at each campus location. Modestino received her Ph.D. in economics from Harvard University where she was also a fellow in the Inequality and Social Policy Program.

MARISOL MORALES (she/her/hers) is the executive director of the Carnegie Elective Classifications and assistant vice president at the American Council on Education. In this role, she provides conceptual leadership and operational oversight to the elective classifications' work in the United States, Australia, and Canada. This includes the collaborative development of and responsibility for all initiatives; oversight and facilitation of relevant national and international advisory committees; conceptualizing and implementing extensive data archives; and developing and enacting a shared vision regarding access to and use of the knowledge produced by the Carnegie Elective Classifications to beneficially guide research, policy, and practice. Prior to this role, Morales was the vice president for network leadership at Campus Compact, the founding director of the Office of Civic and Community Engagement at the University of La Verne, and the associate director of the Steans Center for Community-Based Service Learning and Community Service Studies at DePaul University. She holds an Ed.D. in organizational leadership.

KERRYANN O'MEARA (she/her/hers) is vice president for academic affairs, provost, and dean at Teachers College, Columbia University. She is a professor in the Higher and Postsecondary Education Program in the Organization and Leadership Department. O'Meara's scholarship and leadership are highly integrated and focus on creating a more diverse and inclusive academic workplace. She has designed, tested, and shared evidence-based strategies to remove barriers and improve full participation for scholars from historically minoritized groups with particular attention to faculty hiring, retention, workload, and evaluation. Prior to joining Teachers College, O'Meara served as professor of higher education, distinguished scholar teacher, and special assistant to the provost and to the president for strategic initiatives at the University of Maryland. A prolific scholar and consultant,

APPENDIX B

she has received continuous funding from the National Science Foundation and worked with more than 100 campuses on reforms related to faculty evaluation, workload, hiring, and retention.

ADAM PARRIS (he/him/his) is director of climate resilience at ICF, and an interdisciplinary researcher and knowledge broker with experience developing, applying, and translating science for numerous U.S. states, cities, and local communities. Before joining ICF, he was the deputy director of climate science and services at the Mayor's Office of Climate and Environmental Justice in New York City. Parris catalyzed the development of a Flood Vulnerability Index coupling data on socio-economic stressors and physical flood exposure to help prioritize the city's stormwater improvement and transportation planning efforts. Prior to that, he led the Science and Resilience Institute at Jamaica Bay (SRIJB). While at SRIJB, Parris co-designed Cycles of Resilience, a participatory process to empower communities to develop climate action plans developed with community leaders, civic nonprofits, and scientists, and developed an urban extension program with Sea Grant including community flood monitoring. He has advised federal agencies and numerous states, including California, Maryland, New York, and New Jersey, for which he has been awarded a Presidential GreenGov award as Climate Champion and a National Oceanic and Atmospheric Administration Administrator's Award.

WILLIAM R. PENUEL (he/him/his) is distinguished professor of learning sciences and human development in the Institute of Cognitive Science and School of Education at the University of Colorado Boulder. He designs and studies curriculum materials, assessments, and professional learning experiences for teachers in sciences, technology, engineering, and medicine education, primarily in science. Penuel also investigates how contemplative practices and critical inquiry can support educators in cultivating more compassionate learning environments and schools. A third line of his research focuses on how long-term research-practice partnerships can be organized to address systemic inequities in education systems linked to race, gender and sexual diversity, and language. Penuel is an author of two books on research-practice partnerships, *Creating Research-Practice Partnerships in Education* (Harvard Education Press, 2017) and *Connecting Research and Practice for Educational Improvement* (Routledge, 2018), and co-edited a book on improvement research, *The Foundational Handbook on Improvement Research in Education* (Rowman & Littlefield, 2022). Penuel earned an Ed.M. in counseling processes from Harvard Graduate School of Education and a Ph.D. in developmental psychology from Clark University.

ANGELA G. REYES (she/her/hers) is the founder and executive director of the Detroit Hispanic Development Corporation (DHDC). She was born in Southwest Detroit, where she continues to reside, and is the mother of four, grandmother of eight, and great-grandmother of six children. Reyes has been committed to working in and serving the Latino community for more than 45 years, and founded DHDC from her living room, "because I was tired of burying children." She has developed and managed several successful programs for youth, young adults, and families. Reyes is a founding board member of the Detroit Community-Academic Urban Research Center, which was established in 1995 to address health disparities of residents in Detroit. She has an M.P.H. from the University of Michigan and has been the recipient of several awards for her community work, including the Michiganian of the Year.

MICHAEL RIOS (he/him/his) is vice provost of public scholarship at the University of California, Davis. He is a professor in the Department of Human Ecology and faculty member in the Community Development, Education, and Geography graduate programs. Rios's scholarship focuses on institutional change in higher education, community engagement, community-driven placemaking, and cultural citizenship. He has authored or co-authored more than 20 journal articles and book chapters and has co-edited several books including *Diálogos: Placemaking in Latino Communities* (2013) and *Community Development and Democratic Practice* (2017). Rios was inducted into the Academy of Community Engagement Scholarship in 2024 and is co-founder of the University of California Community Engagement Network. Currently, he is serving a 3-year term on the executive committee of the Association of Public and Land-grant Universities' Commission on Economic and Community Engagement. He holds an M.Arch. degree and an M.S. in city planning from the University of California, Berkeley, and a Ph.D. in political geography from the Pennsylvania State University.

AMY J. SCHULZ (she/her/hers) is a professor in the Department of Health Behavior and Health Education, University of Michigan School of Public Health; University Diversity and Social Transformation Professor, University of Michigan; and a founding member of the Detroit Community-Academic Urban Research Center, a community based participatory research (CBPR) partnership. She is a social scientist with expertise in the joint contributions of social and physical environmental exposures to health inequities, and a leading scholar in the field of CBPR, with extensive experience working collaboratively with community, practice, and academic partners to conduct both etiologic and intervention research. Schulz has served as principal investigator (PI), multi-PI, or co-investigator for multiple CBPR partnerships

APPENDIX B

focused on structural and social determinants of health inequities. She received her M.P.H., M.S.W., and Ph.D. at the University of Michigan.

TOBY SMITH (he/him/his) is senior vice president for government relations and public policy at the Association of American Universities (AAU). In this role he oversees AAU's government relations activities and advocacy efforts, matters related to higher education and science and innovation policy, and AAU's international activities. Smith previously worked as a federal relations representative for the University of Michigan and Massachusetts Institute of Technology. He began his career on Capitol Hill as a legislative assistant to Congressman Bob Traxler (D-MI). Smith writes and speaks widely on issues of science policy. He is the co-author of a book on national science policy, titled *Beyond Sputnik – U.S. Science Policy in the 21st Century*. Smith serves on the Advisory Board for AESIS and is a member of the Council of Experts for the National Science Foundation–sponsored Center for Advancing Research Impact in Society. Smith holds a B.S. degree in general studies from the University of Michigan and an M.A. in legislative affairs from George Washington University.

DOUGLAS A. WATKINS (he/him/his) is the manager of K–12 Science Curriculum and Instruction for Denver Public Schools. His work in that capacity includes partnering with University of Colorado (CU) Boulder learning-science and educational researchers through a research-practice partnership known as inquiryHub (iHub). He is a co-author of the iHub biology and chemistry curricula, as well as a lead author of the pilot versions of two OpenSciEd high school biology curricular units. He supports a team of K–12 science curriculum specialists to provide teachers with professional development for science curriculum use and instructional practice. Watkins has co-designed professional learning workshops for teachers using storylined curricula and has facilitated professional learning experiences with teachers in the Denver metro area and across the country. His areas of scholarly interest include sociolinguistics and teacher learning. He is a recent distinguished graduate of CU Boulder's College of Education Graduate Program, earning an M.A. in learning sciences and human development.

JENNIFER WILDING (she/her/hers) is a community development specialist for the Federal Reserve Bank of Kansas City, where she provides communications, engagement, and research for the community development department. She writes long-form nonfiction for the Kansas City Fed and for Fed Communities, the national website for Federal Reserve community development. Wilding is co-author of *Disconnected: Seven Lessons on Fixing the Digital Divide*, a layperson's guide to putting broadband, devices, and training within reach of a community. She serves on the leadership team of Participatory Action Research for Fed Success and served as project director for an engaged research pilot project. The Kansas City Fed, a nonprofit, and a neighborhood organization joined together to hear from neighborhood residents about broadband internet. This report was shared nationwide. Before joining the Kansas City Fed, Wilding was executive director of a nonprofit consulting firm specializing in public policy and civic engagement.

Appendix C

Participants' Ideas for Metrics of Engaged Research

This appendix presents the ideas that participants contributed for advancing measurement of engaged research at the project, institution, and meta-network levels. The input from in-person and virtual participants were collected using Slido, an online tool that enabled interactive polling. Participants responded to the following prompt:

> If we were to measure what we value, what should we be measuring? What measures most need to be developed? Consider both project and institutional measures, as well as process and outcomes.

Participants' responses are detailed below, organized by nine themes: relationships, trust, competence and capacity for engagement, sustainability, co-production and co-benefits, focus on communities, focus on institutions, focus on meta-networks, and other ideas and resources.[1]

RELATIONSHIPS

- Relationship building (Brian Wampler and Ian Binns)
- Relationships (Jenny Irons)
- Quality of relationships (Michael Rios)
- Relationship satisfaction, quality, longevity (at project/individual level, stories and ratings from all partners) (Elyse Aurbach)

---

[1] In some cases, online participants used only one name to identify themselves.

94   *BUILDING INSTITUTIONAL CAPACITY FOR ENGAGED RESEARCH*

- Additional relationships enabled thanks to the co-produced research (Sonia Hall)
- Community partners' view on the strength and value of the relationships (Sonia Hall)
- Increase in positive feelings between researchers and local communities (Lexi Shultz)
- How do we measure/evaluate how far along a project/relationship is? In other words, when is a relationship ready to apply for funding or other types of support? (Brian Wampler)
- Value of relationship to external partner vs. value of relationship to university-based team (Brian Wampler)
- Relationships in its all their various attributes (Mahmud Farooque)
- Is the partnership resilient and able to survive turnover of members? Is the work and network of relationships strong enough to survive if an influential champion leaves? (Kacy Redd)
- Relationships and trust (Rachel Wurzman)
- Combined qualitative and quantitative metrics of relationship building and connectivity: the number of trainings and professional development not just offered to community but led by community (Eboné Lockett)
- Strength of engagement as research impact (Benjamin Olneck-Brown)
- Activities conducted, number of engagements, formal agreements, number of community members reached, number of community members trained, social outcomes, new resources developed, acceptability of interventions implemented, policy changes, funding distributed to partners, perceptions of co-design and collaboration (Tamara Haegerich)

TRUST

- Trustworthiness (Mary Jo Callan and Faith Uwadiae)
- Measure qualities of a "trustworthy process" (Tim Steffensmeier)
- We should start by asking our partners these questions and being ready to take the time to repair harm, build trust, and establish relationships before asking this question. Depending on the stage of the partnership and past experiences, it is likely that past harm and distrust will result in answers to this question that may not truly reflect the partner's truth—they may just be telling you what they think you want to hear: for example, schools defaulting to "student achievement" because that is what they are told by their state. (Kim Wright)
- I really like the "trustworthiness" reframe. I would add that one concept in learning sciences that is important is politicized trust,

which acknowledges the location of trust building within networks of power. (Bill Penuel)

- People feel safe in a process as a measure of collaboration (Adam Parris)
- Trust for research can come from support for science (and understanding of science) by religious communities. The putative "conflict" between religion and science needs to be addressed. (John L. Burch)
- Trust and community empowerment: awareness, agency, action (Marisol Morales)
- How many activities are initiated by the community? (Marisol Morales)
- How does higher ed institution become a preferential partner because trust exists? (Marisol Morales)
- Measure depth and pervasiveness of partnership (Marisol Morales)
- Measure preparation of students and university-affiliated folks to enter community respectfully and humbly (Marisol Morales)
- As a citizen myself, in an effort to better set diverse, equitable, inclusive, and accessible targets for allocating our limited resources, I feel improvements could be made to assess the presence of secure spaces to have vulnerable conversations about community needs and values representative of local demographics and geographies (Charles Smeltzer)
- Trustworthiness and systems engagement with partners toward actionable solutions and change (Nadine Barrett)

COMPETENCE AND CAPACITY FOR ENGAGEMENT

- Engagement competencies (Elise Cappella)
- Engagement supports (trainings, mentoring, incentives, coaching, recognition) (Elise Cappella)
- Cultural humility (Michael Rios)
- We need to determine what qualities are really required to do community-engaged research, such as trustworthiness, and then ensure that funders, professors, and universities are really looking for and assessing the level of this quality when anyone from their organization (or someone they are going to fund, in the funder's case) is doing work with communities (Katie)

SUSTAINABILITY

- Institutional track record for delivering on sustainability in a variety of ways, including internal sustaining, partner sustaining, embedding, spinoff into new independent organizations (Jessica Bennett)

- Is the intervention attracting sustainable/ongoing funding? (Kacy Redd)
- Retention and advancement of engaged researchers throughout the academic career path: undergrad through full professor (Erhardt Graeff)
- Map where possible to U.N. Sustainable Development Goals, including good health and well-being, reducing inequalities, and partnerships (Arthur Ellis)
- Sustainability of partnerships to maximize an approach that starts with partnership and not the specific funding opportunity. We often blame funders for making us approach community partners at the 11th hour or after an investigation is fully planned. If we focus instead on cultivating enduring partnerships, research projects, questions, and funding proposals will flow from those. (Mary Jo Callan)
- Policy change; community ownership and sustainability of intervention and programs: measures have to be tailored to what the program was designed to affect, which is hard to aggregate (Laurie Van Egeren)

CO-PRODUCTION AND CO-BENEFITS

- Specific changes that the co-produced research informed, influenced, or amplified (Sonia Hall)
- For all outcome-based measures: is there alignment in view of progress and impact among all partners? (Sonia Hall)
- Decisions that were changed in response to the co-produced research results *and* in response to the co-production process (Sonia Hall)
- Co-develop measures of the outcomes that community members care about and outcomes they can use for advocacy beyond the research project (Heidi Schweingruber)
- Measures of partnership quality (Laurie Van Egeren)
- Change and evolution in research questions and approaches through the co-production process (Sonia Hall)
- The co-creation of research questions to address, as well as methodologies: that is, the development of a collaborative research agenda is an outcome in itself (Lexi Shultz)
- Increased institutional recognition of and investment in co-production and community science (Lexi Shultz)
- Increased participation and sense of co-ownership (Nova)
- Numbers and percentages of research project presentations at academic and public events that are led or co-presented by community partners (with funding for their travel and time included in grants) (Erhardt Graeff)

APPENDIX C

- Partnership equity and effectiveness, including in communication, resources, decision making, engagement, and influence (Elise Cappella)
- Perceptions and experience related to equity and benefit of a partnership (Mary Jo Callan)
- Measurement of how accurately partners feel that their experiences and expertise were captured and represented by researchers (Deondra Rose)
- We should measure experiential outcomes related to the processes engaged in, for both researchers and community members. Measures that can influence change of practice and research are important. (Douglas A. Watkins)
- Components of the participatory process and measure each of these (Susanna Campbell)
- Engaging the community in identifying the problem, developing the measures, and developing the solutions (Nadine Barrett)
- Equity in partnerships and collaborations (Nadine Barrett)
- Actual systems change informed and co-developed with community expertise (Nadine Barrett)
- Level of agreement that a collaborative endeavor empowered participants to take action (Adam Parris)
- For all outcome-based measures, is there alignment in view of progress and impact among all partners? (Sonia Hall)

FOCUS ON COMMUNITIES

- Whether the community thinks the problems they prioritize are being addressed (Heidi Schweingruber)
- Community capacity building (Michael Rios)
- Needs of the community and barriers to meeting those needs (Jo)
- For a specific focus—water quality, for example—the community sees improvement or has specific data they can use to push for improvements (Lexi Shultz)
- Measures of whether and how the university is providing learning opportunities for researchers to develop capacities to work with communities (Heidi Schweingruber)
- Implementation measures, such as RE-AIM,[2] with a focus on community populations so we start getting at sustainability of interventions in communities (Jeanette Waxmonsky)
- At institutional level, where community partnerships are happening, how they are brokered, who is involved (and their satisfaction), relationship with discipline, etc. (Elyse Aurbach)

---

[2] Reach-Effectiveness-Adoption-Implementation-Maintenance; see https://re-aim.org/

- Level and diversity of engagement by community partners, as a proxy for whether they see the value in the partnership (Sonia Hall)
- Agency of community partners in affecting change (Sonia Hall)
- Subjective quality of life of the community: to analyze "soft" measures, well-being, feelings of people, including qualitative measures (Gerlinde Kristahn)
- Measures impacts that undergird economic development/prosperity (Tim Steffensmeier)
- First need to capture what communities see of value in a partnership with research institutions/researchers. Measure whether those needs/objectives are being met. They don't always want data and research. (Elsa Falkenburger)
- Outputs and products for the community, and whether they are used and applied by the community in pursuit of their goals (Sonia Hall)
- Measure the stabilizers created with community input. How effective were they in instilling ownership and stability? (John James)
- Improved quality of life, sustainability, empowerment of communities (Nova)
- We need to move beyond activity to actual impact. Numbers are important, but we need to know if what we are doing actually makes a difference in people's lives. (Susan Renoe)
- Impact on public health outcomes, impact on democratic agency: Do people feel more empowered to participate in democracy more broadly as a result of participating in engaged research? Creation and value of new collaborative relationships (Adam Levine)
- Community and collaborator perceptions of whether and how the research effort addressed their needs (Kaytee Canfield)
- Change in quality of actions taken or decisions made, using metrics the user organization employs (Lawrence Friedl)

FOCUS ON INSTITUTIONS

- Measures and benchmarks for institutional change: What does an engaged university look like in this moment? What should be seen as foundational expectations vs. more contextually situated? (Benjamin Olneck-Brown)
- The proportion of engaged research projects at our institution that were catalyzed by a community-identified agenda or use-case in comparison to the number that come from an institutionally identified agenda or use-case (Lina Dostilio)
- Is the partnership being shared with decision makers—including state legislatures, community leaders, institutional president,

APPENDIX C 99

donors, alumni, or industry leaders—in press releases, briefings, or other dissemination venues? (Kacy Redd)
- Understanding how to align individual perceptions of individuals in the institution to the institutional level (Prajakta Adsul)
- How do we capture if a community-based activity promotes the values of the institution? (Brian Wampler)
- Policy and infrastructure support: evaluate institutional changes that support community-engaged research, such as the creation of offices, staffing, and funding dedicated to such initiatives. This might include tracking changes in policy that facilitate community access to university resources. (Richard A. Tankersley)
- Long-term engagement: measure the sustainability of community partnerships beyond individual projects. Metrics could include the number of multiyear community projects supported by the institution or the renewal rates of community partnership agreements. (Richard A. Tankersley)
- Cultural competence: monitor the institution's progress in fostering an environment that respects and incorporates diverse cultural perspectives. This could be measured through diversity and inclusion training participation rates and feedback on institutional climate from community partners. (Richard A. Tankersley)
- Number of academic institutions offering public-facing reports specifically touting engaged scholarship and community partnerships (Erhardt Graeff)
- Outlets for researchers other than publications (Lexi Shultz)
- Measure how institutional resources—such as dollars, in kind contributions, power—are accessible or being leveraged for community priorities and community benefit (Elsa Falkenburger)
- Tracking university investments in support for community-engaged research—such as payments to community members, training of researchers, and staff to support partnership building (Heidi Schweingruber)
- Percentage of grants awarded that offer significant time and resources for relationship building and compensating non-academic partners (Erhardt Graeff)
- Also need to better capture context and contextual conditions within an organization (Prajakta Adsul)
- Institutional culture and support for this and other work (e.g., DEI [diversity, equity, and inclusion]) via surveys, focus groups, etc. (Elyse Aurbach)
- Revision of P&T [promotion and tenure] to reflect the kind of work needed for community engagement and the time it takes to do it well (Heidi Schweingruber)

FOCUS ON META-NETWORKS

- We need measures that are accessible to researchers, practitioners, and partners. This includes evaluations and assessment measures, both qualitative and quantitative. These can be held at the national or institutional level so there is consistency in utilizing promising practices. (Susan Renoe)
- Many measures already exist but we aren't aware of across disciplines: How can our meta-network support cross-fertilization on the measurement and adaptation side? (Emily Ozer)
- Review and assess portfolio and quality of research and community partnerships. Measure number of grants and programs funded with community partnerships. Monitor across the depth of community partnerships on a continuum from being involved as a part of an advisory board or participating in a focus group to serving as a PI [principal investigator] or co-PI. (Nadine Barrett)

OTHER IDEAS AND RESOURCES

- The research in question moves from usable to used; there is a documentable approach and learning for uptake of usable data. (Lexi Shultz)
- Framework for evaluation of RPPs [requests for preliminary proposals] that we've iterated since 2017 and developed both associated measures *and* sense-making routines for them: five dimensions relate to trust, supporting partner organizations in meeting *their* outcomes, co-involvement in research, producing original research, and building capacity for ongoing joint work[3] (Bill Penuel)
- Increased participation in STEM [science, technology, engineering, and mathematics]-identifying individuals (Lexi Shultz)
- We look at epistemic justice by gathering data that are easily collected in the end of class about students' experience of the classroom and use them systemically to try and address the education debt owed to racially minoritized students, and also girls and gender nonbinary students.[4] (Bill Penuel)
- Engage evaluators throughout project life-cycles to assess and substantiate impacts in social and economic terms (Lawrence Friedl)

---

[3] See https://nnerpp.rice.edu/rpp-effectiveness-and-health-tool-kit/

[4] Penuel, W. R., & Watkins, D. A. (2019). Assessment to promote equity and epistemic justice: A use-case of a research-practice partnership in science education. *The ANNALS of the American Academy of Political and Social Science, 683*(1), 201–216. https://doi.org/10.1177/0002716219843249